THE GREAT MOVIE MUSICAL SONGBOOK

Notes on the films by David Fantle

ISBN 0-7935-3364-3

HAL•LEONARD®
CORPORATION
7777 W. BLUEMOUND RD. P.O. BOX 13819 MILWAUKEE, WI 53213

Visit Hal Leonard Online at
www.halleonard.com

CONTENTS
(alphabetical by movie title)

CONTENTS
(alphabetical by song title)

AN AMERICAN IN PARIS

1951, MGM

music by George Gershwin; lyrics by Ira Gershwin; screenplay by Alan Jay Lerner; produced by Arthur Freed; directed by Vincente Minnelli; choreography by Gene Kelly; photography by Alfred Gilks & John Alton

major cast members: Gene Kelly, Leslie Caron, Oscar Levant, Georges Guetary, Nina Foch, Benny Carter Orch., Andre Charisse, Eugene Borden, Martha Barnattre, Ann Codee, Dudley Field Malone

songs: Embraceable You; By Strauss; I Got Rhythm; Tra-La-La; Love Is Here to Stay; I'll Build a Stairway to Paradise (lyric with B.G. DeSylva); Piano Concerto in F (third movement); 'S Wonderful; An American in Paris (ballet)

featured song in this collection: Love Is Here to Stay

Take an ex-G.I. who is an aspiring painter (Gene Kelly), place him in post World War II Paris and get him entangled in a love triangle with Leslie Caron (in her film debut) and Georges Guetary. Add nine songs (including two instrumental pieces) from the George and Ira Gershwin songbook and a supporting cast that includes Oscar Levant and Nina Foch. Title the film *An American in Paris* and you've mixed together the ingredients for a success. "Love is Here to Stay," the last song written by George Gershwin before his untimely death in 1937, is danced with elegance by Kelly and Caron on the banks of the River Seine. The pièce de resistance of the film is the 17-minute ballet, danced to Gershwin's *An American in Paris* and set against the canvases of Dufy, Renoir, Utrillo, Rousseau, Van Gogh and Toulouse-Lautrec. *An American in Paris* earned six Academy Awards in 1951, including best picture (an honor bestowed on a musical only nine times) and a special Oscar to Kelly for his artistic contribution to the field of film dance. Available on video.

ANNIE GET YOUR GUN

1950, MGM

music & lyrics by Irving Berlin; screenplay by Sidney Sheldon; produced by Arthur Freed; directed by George Sidney; choreography by Robert Alton; photography by Charles Rosher

major cast members: Betty Hutton, Howard Keel, Louis Calhern, J. Carrol Naish, Edward Arnold, Keenan Wynn, Benay Venuta, Clinton Sundberg, Andre Charlot, Mae Clarke, Chief Yowlachie, Bradley Mora, Diana Dick, Susan Odin, Eleanor Brown

songs: Colonel Buffalo Bill; Doin' What Comes Natur'lly; The Girl That I Marry; You Can't Get a Man With a Gun; There's No Business Like Show Business; They Say It's Wonderful; My Defenses Are Down; I'm an Indian, Too; I Got the Sun in the Morning; Anything You Can Do

featured song in this collection: Anything You Can Do

Ethel Merman owned the title role of Irving Berlin's 1946 hit *Annie Get Your Gun* on the Broadway stage, where it played for 1,147 performances. But when MGM bought the rights (at a then staggering cost of $700,000) it had only one singing actress in mind to play the tomboyish, "Can't Get a Man With a Gun" Annie Oakley: Judy Garland. Garland recorded the vocals and shooting had begun under the direction of Busby Berkeley when artistic differences developed between star and director. Berkeley was fired. Soon Berkeley's replacement, Charles Walters, also departed. Finally problems with Garland forced her exit. Following a five-month delay, the production resumed under the direction of George Sidney and starring Paramount's musical-comedy queen Betty Hutton and newcomer Howard Keel. The story follows sharpshooter Oakley, her rise to fame in Buffalo Bill's Wild West Show and her romance with fellow marksman Frank Butler (Keel). After a falling out, Annie throws a challenge match against Butler to win him back. Berlin's ode to one-up manship, "Anything You Can Do" provides a lyrical "battle of the sexes" between Hutton and Keel.

THE BAND WAGON

1953, MGM

music by Arthur Schwartz; lyrics by Howard Dietz; screenplay by Betty Comden and Adolph Green; produced by Arthur Freed; directed by Vincente Minnelli; choreography by Michael Kidd; photography by Harry Jackson

major cast members: Fred Astaire, Cyd Charisse, Oscar Levant, Nanette Fabray, Jack Buchanan, James Mitchell, Thurston Hall, Ava Gardner (cameo), Julie Newmar, Matt Mattox, LeRoy Daniels

songs: By Myself; A Shine on Your Shoes; That's Entertainment; Dancing in the Dark; Something to Remember You By; High and Low; I Love Louisa, New Sun in the Sky; I Guess I'll Have to Change My Plan; Louisiana Hayride; Triplets; The Girl Hunt Ballet (narration written by Alan Jay Lerner)

featured song in this collection: That's Entertainment

The Band Wagon is a movie musical feast showcasing the song catalogue of Arthur Schwartz and Howard Dietz. The film tells the story of a washed up song-and-dance-man (Fred Astaire) who returns to Broadway to jump start his flagging career. His comeback vehicle gets sidetracked when the show's director, Jeffrey Cordova (played by the debonair British singer-dancer Jack Buchanan), wants to turn the musical comedy into an updated version of **Faust**. Oscar Levant and Nanette Fabray play the playwrights who helplessly watch their words get mutilated by Cordova. There's the inevitable dramatic tension when the hoofer Astaire meets his co-star, ballerina Cyd Charisse. Don't worry. It all works out in the end — the show, which is on its way to becoming a flop, is rescued by the cast and becomes a smash. Astaire and Charisse become compatible in more than just dance. The film shares the name (but no other similarities) with a 1931 Schwartz-Dietz revue, which starred Astaire and his sister Adele. "That's Entertainment," the one new song written for the film, has become a show business anthem. Available on video.

BELLS ARE RINGING
1960, MGM

music by Jule Styne; lyrics and screenplay by Betty Comden & Adolph Green; produced by Arthur Freed; directed by Vincente Minnelli; choreography by Charles O'Curran; photography by Milton Krasner

major cast members: Judy Holliday, Dean Martin, Fred Clark, Eddie Foy Jr., Jean Stapleton, Dort Clark, Frank Gorshin, Bernie West, Gerry Mulligan, Hal Linden

songs: It's a Perfect Relationship; Do It Yourself; It's a Simple Little System; Better Than a Dream; I Met a Girl; Just in Time; Drop That Name; The Party's Over; I'm Going Back

featured song in this collection: Just in Time

The 1956 Broadway musical **Bells Are Ringing**, provided a star turn for actress Judy Holliday (who had earlier scored success for her stage and film portrayal of the scatterbrained blond Billie Dawn in **Born Yesterday**). The script, written by her friends and former nightclub partners Betty Comden and Adolph Green, tells the story of a big-hearted but nosy answering service operator who does good deeds for her clients. Among them is a handsome playwright she falls in love with. The show was transferred to the screen in 1960 with Holliday again starring. In the film, Dean Martin plays the playwright. The show is probably best remembered for the Jule Styne, Comden and Green standards "Just in Time" (sung as a love song between Holliday and Martin) and "The Party's Over." The film was Holliday's last screen appearance. She died in 1965 at the age of 43. Available on video.

THE BIG BROADCAST OF 1938
1938, Paramount

music by Ralph Rainger, lyrics by Leo Robin; screenplay by Walter DeLeon, Francis Martin, Ken Englund; produced by Harlan Thompson; directed by Mitchel Leisen; choreography by LeRoy Prinz; photography by Harry Fishbeck, Gordon Jennings

major cast members: W.C. Fields, Bob Hope, Dorothy Lamour, Shirley Ross, Martha Raye, Lynne Overman, Leif Erickson, Ben Blue, Grace Bradley, Patricia Wilder, Shep Fields Orch., Tito Guizar, Kirsten Flagstad

songs: You Took the Words Right Out of My Heart; Brunnhilde's Battle Cry (Wagner); Thanks for the Memory; Mama, That Moon Is Here Again; The Waltz Lives On

featured song in this collection: Thanks for the Memory

In *The Big Broadcast of 1938* the bulb-nosed comedian W.C. Fields meets the ski-nosed comic Bob Hope. The fourth and final film in a series celebrating the nation's love affair with radio provides some clever comic turns from Fields as he cavorts on a golf course and tears up the felt (literally) on a billiard table. The movie marked Hope's feature film debut. The young comedian from Cleveland had just made a name for himself on Broadway in such shows as *Roberta* and *Red, Hot and Blue*. The gags are strung around a plot that concerns a transatlantic race between two ocean liners. The "broadcast" part of the story has Hope delivering daily ship-to-shore radio updates on the race. The musical highlight: Hope and Shirley Ross singing the Oscar winner (and forever after Hope theme song) "Thanks for the Memory."

CABARET

1972, Allied Artists & ABC

music by John Kander; lyrics by Fred Ebb; screenplay by Jay Presson Allen; produced by Cy Feuer; directed and choreography by Bob Fosse; photography by Geoffrey Unsworth

major cast members: Liza Minnelli, Michael York, Helmut Griem, Joel Grey, Marisa Berenson, Fritz Wepper, Elizabeth Neumann-Viertel, Oliver Collignon, Angelika Koch, Louise Quick

songs: Willkommen; Mein Herr; Maybe This Time; Money, Money; Two Ladies; Hieraten; Tomorrow Belongs to Me; If You Could See Her; Cabaret

featured song in this collection: Money, Money

Director Bob Fosse set out to depict the decadence, decay and perverse atmosphere of pre-World War II Berlin when he adapted the successful 1966 stage show *Cabaret* for film. British actress Jill Haworth starred in the stage version despite a strong lobbying effort by songwriters John Kander

and Fred Ebb to cast Liza Minnelli in the lead role of the fun-seeking, yet vulnerable Sally Bowles. Fosse "Americanized" the Bowles character and cast Minnelli in his 1972 film. The role of the Master of Ceremonies was reprised by Tony award-winner Joel Grey. "Money Money" was written especially for the screen version, a song about greed sung by Minnelli and Grey, who both won Oscars for their portrayals. Available on video.

CALL ME MADAM

1953, 20th Century-Fox

music & lyrics by Irving Berlin; screenplay by Arthur Sheekman; produced by Sol C. Siegel; directed by Walter Lang; choreography by Robert Alton; photography by Leon Shamroy

major cast members: Ethel Merman, George Sanders, Donald O'Conner, Vera-Ellen, Billy DeWolfe, Helmut Dantine; Walter Slezak, Ludwig Stossel, Charles Dingle, Walter Woolf King, Johnny Downs

songs: The Hostess With the Mostes'; Can You Use Any Money Today?; Marrying for Love; It's a Lovely Day Today; That International Rag; The Ocarina; What Chance Have I With Love?; The Best Thing for You; Something to Dance About; You're Just in Love

featured song in this collection: (I Wonder Why) You're Just in Love

Irving Berlin's *Call Me Madam* is based on the life of Perle Mesta, a Washington D.C. hostess named by President Truman as Ambassador to Luxembourg. The 1950 musical written for Ethel Merman has the society maven as Ambassador to the fictionalized principality of Lichtenburg where she becomes romantically entangled with another foreign diplomat. Along the way she dispenses some musical advice to her lovelorn aide (Donald O'Connor on film) with the duet, "You're Just in Love." The song was inserted into the stage show after its tryout in New Haven when Merman complained to Berlin that the second act was lacking a show-stopper. *Call Me Madam* was one of all too few film musicals to star Broadway legend "la Merman."

CAN-CAN

1960, 20th Century-Fox

music & lyrics by Cole Porter; screenplay by Dorothy Kingsley & Charles Lederer; produced by Jack Cummings; directed by Walter Lang; choreography by Hermes Pan; photography by William Daniels

major cast members: Frank Sinatra, Shirley MacLaine, Maurice Chevalier, Louis Jourdan, Juliet Prowse, Marcel Dalio, Leon Belasco

songs: C'est Magnifique; You Do Something to Me; Let's Do It; It's All Right With Me; Live and Let Live; Come Along With Me; Just One of Those Things

featured song in this collection: You Do Something to Me

Can-Can followed the 1958 Oscar-winning success of *Gigi*. The 1960 film was adapted from Cole Porter's 1950 stage musical. To accommodate a star-studded cast of Frank Sinatra, Shirley MacLaine, Louis Jourdan and Maurice Chevalier (the last two were holdovers from *Gigi*), the story was extensively rewritten for the film. The celluloid version concerns the efforts of a newly appointed judge (Jourdan) to suppress the scandalous dance known as the can-can from being performed in a Parisian cabaret owned by MacLaine. Sinatra plays a lawyer who defends MacLaine's right to can-can. Jourdan plays Sinatra's rival for MacLaine (he sings to her Porter's 1929 song "You Do Something to Me"), and Chevalier is cast as the likable older judge who looks the other way in matters of the can-can. The film received some extra publicity mileage when Soviet Premier Nikita Khrushchev visited the set and watched the final dance sequence being filmed. Available on video.

CAREFREE

1938, RKO Radio Pictures

music & lyrics by Irving Berlin; screenplay by Ernest Pagano & Allan Scott; produced by Pandro S. Berman; directed by Mark Sandrich; choreography by Hermes Pan (Fred Astaire uncredited); photography by Robert de Grasse

major cast members: Fred Astaire, Ginger Rogers, Ralph Bellamy, Luella Gear, Jack Carson, Clarence Kolb, Franklin Pangborn, Hattie McDaniel, Walter Kingsford, Kay Sutton

songs: I Used to Be Color Blind; The Yarn; Change Partners

featured song in this collection: Change Partners

After a one-film hiatus on his own (*A Damsel in Distress*), *Carefree* reunited Fred Astaire with Ginger Rogers (who had made three consecutive films without Astaire). *Carefree* is the eighth film in the celebrated series and was really a star turn for Rogers, who had an opportunity to display her comic flair. Astaire plays a psychiatrist who uses hypnosis to convince his patient (Rogers) that she really loves him, not her fiancé, Ralph Bellamy. Irving Berlin had written the song "Change Partners" a few years earlier in anticipation of Astaire's eventual split with Rogers. Instead, the song was used to woo Rogers away from Bellamy and back into Astaire's arms. Astaire's artistry never ceases to amaze. What he does with a golf club and balls in the dance number "Since They Turned Loch Lomond into Swing" is enough to cause any weekend duffer consternation. Available on video.

DADDY LONG LEGS

1955, 20th Century-Fox

music & lyrics by Johnny Mercer; screenplay by Phoebe & Henry Ephron; produced by Samuel G. Engel; directed by Jean Negulesco; choreography by David Robel, Roland Petit (Fred Astaire uncredited); photography by Leon Shamroy

major cast members: Fred Astaire, Leslie Caron, Terry Moore, Thelma Ritter, Fred Clark, Ralph Dumke, Larry Keating, Ray Anthony Orch.

songs: History of the Beat; Dream; Sluefoot; Something's Gotta Give *featured song in this collection:* Something's Gotta Give

The story for the 1955 film is taken from a 1912 novel written by Jean Webster concerning a wealthy businessman (Fred Astaire), who to avoid gossip about his motives, becomes the anonymous sponsor of a young orphan girl's education. The girl's only sighting of her benefactor is a spidery shadow, hence she refers to him as her "daddy long legs." The two eventually meet and fall in love. In the film, the American orphan was changed to French so studio head Darryl Zanuck could cast Leslie Caron, hot off her screen successes in *An American in Paris* and *Lili*. To reconcile the 32-year age discrepancy between the suitor and the object of his affections, songwriter Johnny Mercer (in a rare turn as both composer and lyricist) bridged the age gap with the song "Something's Gotta Give" — "When an irresistible force such as you, meets an *old* immovable object like me."

A DAMSEL IN DISTRESS

1937, RKO Radio Pictures

music by George Gershwin; lyrics by Ira Gershwin; screenplay by P.G. Wodehouse, Ernest Pagano, S.K. Lauren; produced by Pandro S. Berman; directed by George Stevens; choreography by Hermes Pan (Fred Astaire uncredited); photography by Joseph August

major cast members: Fred Astaire, George Burns, Gracie Allen, Joan Fontaine, Reginald Gardiner, Ray Noble, Constance Collier, Montagu Love

songs: I Can't Be Bothered Now; The Jolly Tar and the Milkmaid; Stiff Upper Lip; Things Are Looking Up; A Foggy Day; Nice Work If You Can Get It

featured song in this collection: A Foggy Day

After seven successive films together, it was time to call the whole thing off (at least temporarily) for America's most celebrated dance team, Fred Astaire and Ginger Rogers. Astaire's first Ginger-less movie was based on a 1919 P.G. Wodehouse novel that the author adapted for the London stage in 1928 called *A Damsel in Distress*. The film version concerns an American dancer (Astaire) appearing in London who goes to the romantic rescue of Lady Alyce (played by the non-singing and non-dancing actress Joan Fontaine) in a countryside castle. Astaire introduces the Gershwin classic "A Foggy Day" not in London-Town, but on the grounds of the castle. The imaginative fun-house dance with Astaire, George Burns and Gracie Allen won choreographer Hermes Pan an Academy Award. Available on video.

EASTER PARADE

1948, MGM

music & lyrics by Irving Berlin; screenplay by Sidney Sheldon, Frances Goodrich, Albert Hackett; produced by Arthur Freed; directed by Charles Walters; choreography by Robert Alton (Charles Walters, Fred Astaire uncredited); photography by Harry Stradling

major cast members: Judy Garland, Fred Astaire, Peter Lawford, Ann Miller, Jules Munchin, Clinton Sundberg, Richard Beavers, Benay Venuta, Lola Albright, Dee Turnell

songs: Happy Easter; Drum Crazy; It Only Happens When I Dance With You; Everybody's Doin' It; I Want to Go Back to Michigan; Beautiful Faces Need Beautiful Clothes; A Fella With an Umbrella; I Love a Piano; Snookey Ookums; Ragtime Violin; When the Midnight Choo-Choo Leaves for Alabam'; Shaking the Blues Away; Steppin' Out With My Baby; A Couple of Swells; The Girl on the Magazine Cover; Better Luck Next Time; Easter Parade

featured song in this collection: Steppin' Out With My Baby

From the opening shot of Fred Astaire's lithesome jaunt down New York's 5th Avenue, you know you're in for a musical treat. Astaire came out of a two-year retirement (after original star Gene Kelly broke his ankle in a touch football game) to co-star with Judy Garland in *Easter Parade*. The story, set in 1912, follows the troubles of vaudeville star Don Hewes (Astaire) who suddenly must break in a new partner after the old one (Ann Miller) abruptly departs to star in a Ziegfeld show. To prove that he can dance with anyone, he randomly picks Hannah Brown (Garland) out of the chorus at a cafe floor show. Peter Lawford provides some romantic tension as Astaire's playboy friend. It all gets sorted out in the end, and the team of Astaire and Garland become a show business sensation and the hit of New York's annual Easter Parade. Irving Berlin wrote seven new songs for the picture, including "Steppin' Out With My Baby," a slow motion dance by Astaire superimposed in front of the chorus dancing at regular speed. Available on video.

piece of film making for its day — an aerial floor show with scantily clad chorines doing a Rockettes-style routine to the title tune while strapped to the wings of an airplane. The film gave audiences a taste of the Astaire-Rogers magic, but the best was yet to come. Available on video.

FOLLOW THE FLEET

1936, RKO Radio Pictures

music & lyrics by Irving Berlin; screenplay by Dwight Taylor & Allan Scott; produced by Pandro S. Berman; directed by Mark Sandrich; choreography by Hermes Pan (Fred Astaire uncredited); photography by David Abel

major cast members: Fred Astaire, Ginger Rogers, Randolph Scott, Harriet Hilliard, Astrid Allwyn, Lucille Ball, Betty Grable, Joy Hodges, Tony Martin, Frank Jenks, Ray Mayer, Russell Hicks, Harry Beresford, Addison Randall, Herbert Rawlinson

songs: We Saw the Sea; Let Yourself Go; Get Thee Behind Me, Satan; I'd Rather Lead A Band; But Where Are You?; I'm Putting All My Eggs in One Basket; Let's Face the Music and Dance

featured song in this collection: Let's Face the Music and Dance

After the success of **Top Hat**, studio executives decided it was time to revise the Fred Astaire-Ginger Rogers formula a bit. Translation: strip Astaire of his top hat, white tie and tails (at least for most of the film) and make him a gum-chewing gob. The film, about two seaman (Astaire and Randolph Scott) and their landlocked girls (Rogers and Harriet Hilliard before she became Mrs. Ozzie Nelson) resembles a filmed version of a double date. The film did have a tuneful Irving Berlin score going for it. In a dance hall competition, Astaire teams with Rogers and cuts loose with the song "Let Yourself Go." Astaire dons the formal attire for the film's finale, the lilting "Let's Face the Music and Dance." The song, staged as part of a benefit show, was a real-life pain for Astaire. The heavily beaded sleeves on Roger's gown pummeled him during the number's 14 takes. If you look closely, you'll see Lucille Ball, Betty Grable and Tony Martin in bit parts. Available on video.

FLYING DOWN TO RIO

1933, RKO Radio Pictures

music by Vincent Youmans; lyrics by Edward Eliscu & Gus Kahn; screenplay by Cyril Hume, H.W. Hanemann, Erwin Gelsey; produced by Louis Brock; directed by Thornton Freeland; choreography by Dave Gould, Hermes Pan (Fred Astaire uncredited); photography by J. Roy Hunt

major cast members: Delores Del Rio, Gene Raymond, Raul Roulien, Ginger Rogers, Fred Astaire, Blanche Friderici, Franklin Pangborn, Eric Blore, Etta Moten, Betty Furness, Mary Kornman

songs: Music Makes Me; The Carioca; Orchids in the Moonlight; Flying Down to Rio

featured song in this collection: The Carioca

Flying Down to Rio has an important place in film history. It forged the legendary on-screen partnership between Fred Astaire and Ginger Rogers, and with the words "We'll show 'em a thing or three," said by Rogers, it introduced film audiences to the pairs' first musical number together, the rumba-style "Carioca." Astaire and Rogers weren't even given top billing. The credits list them behind Delores Del Rio, Gene Raymond and Raul Roulien. Del Rio plays the daughter of a South American hotel owner. Her suitor, musician/pilot (Raymond), flies down to Rio to woo her away from countryman Roulien. The film's climax is a dazzling

FOR ME AND MY GAL

1942, MGM

screenplay by Richard Sherman, Fred Finklehoffe, Sid Silvers; produced by Arthur Freed; directed by Busby Berkeley; choreography by Bobby Connolly (Gene Kelly uncredited); photography by William Daniels

major cast members: Judy Garland, Gene Kelly, George Murphy; Marta Eggerth, Ben Blue, Richard Quine, Keenan Wynn, Stephen McNally *songs:* Oh, You Beautiful Doll (Nat Ayer-Seymour Brown); For Me and My Gal (George Meyer-Edgar Leslie, E. Ray Goetz); When You Wore a Tulip (Percy Wenrich-Jack Mahoney); After You've Gone (Henry Creamoer-Turner Layton); Till We Meet Again (Richard Whiting-Raymond Egan); Ballin' the Jack (Chris Smith-Jim Burris)

featured song in this collection: For Me and My Gal

Gene Kelly became a star by playing the ingratiating cad Joey Evans in Rodgers and Hart's 1940 Broadway production of *Pal Joey.* So it wasn't a real stretch for Kelly when he was cast to play a similar character in his film debut, "For Me and My Gal." It's the story of two vaudevillians (Judy Garland and Kelly), their climb to stardom and Kelly's insatiable desire to play the Palace Theatre, the pinnacle for any vaudeville star. Kelly doesn't let anything get in his way, even a draft notice. To avoid serving, he slams his fingers in a steamer trunk. Since Garland's brother (Richard Quine) made the ultimate sacrifice — he fought and died — it makes Kelly's act seem that much more despicable and it leads to the inevitable breakup with Garland. A repentant Kelly decides to entertain the troops, and in the course of his overseas stay, he saves an ambulance convoy from ambush. It all ends predictably when the two reunite — at the Palace. The title song is sung and danced with exuberance by Garland and Kelly. Available on video.

FUNNY GIRL

1968, Columbia & Rastar

music by Jule Styne; lyrics by Bob Merrill; screenplay by Isobel Lennart; produced by Ray Stark; directed by William Wyler (Herbert Ross uncredited); choreography by Herbert Ross; photography by Harry Stradling

major cast members: Barbra Streisand, Omar Sharif, Kay Medford, Anne Francis, Walter Pidgeon, Lee Allen, Mae Questel, Tommy Rall

songs: I'm the Greatest Star; If a Girl Isn't Pretty; Roller Skate Rag; His Love Makes Me Beautiful; I'd Rather Be Blue Over You (Fred Fisher-Billy Rose); Second Hand Rose (James Hanley-Grant Clarke); People; You Are Woman, I Am Man; Don't Rain on My Parade; Sadie, Sadie; The Swan; Funny Girl; My Man (Maurice Yvain-Channing Pollock)

featured song in the collection: Funny Girl

It was producer Ray Stark's idea to stage a musical about his mother-in-law, entertainer Fanny Brice. A relatively unknown singer from Brooklyn, Barbra Streisand, was not his first choice to play the part. When negotiations with his original choice, Anne Bancroft, fell through, Streisand got the nod, launching her remarkable career when the show opened on Broadway in 1964. The 1968 film version also starred Streisand in her film debut. *Funny Girl* is the backstage

musical story of Ziegfeld star Brice, her rise to fame and her stormy relationship with gambler/embezzler Nick Arnstein (played on screen by Omar Sharif). Of the sixteen songs in the original Jule Styne-Bob Merrill score, seven, including the classic "People," were retained in the screen version. The title song, newly written for the film, is sung by Streisand during a somber moment after she watches her husband go off to prison. A sequel to the film, *Funny Lady* (again starring Streisand) was made in 1975. Available on video.

42ND STREET

1933, Warner Brothers

music by Harry Warren; lyrics by Al Dubin; screenplay by James Seymour, Rian James; produced by Darryl F. Zanuck; directed by Lloyd Bacon (Mervyn LeRoy, uncredited); choreography by Busby Berkeley; photography by Sol Polito

major cast members: Ruby Keeler, Warner Baxter, Bebe Daniels, George Brent, Dick Powell, Ginger Rogers, Una Merkel, Guy Kibbee, Ned Sparks

songs: You're Getting to Be a Habit With Me; Shuffle Off to Buffalo; Young and Healthy; Forty-Second Street

featured song in this collection: Forty-Second Street

42nd Street is one of the most important musical films ever made. In the early years of sound pictures, the market was glutted with musicals, peaking in the year 1930. By 1931 musicals no longer drew audiences, and in 1932 Hollywood only released a dozen or so musicals. Then, in February of 1933, *42nd Street* hit the theaters, and was such a runaway hit that it single-handedly revived the entire genre of movie musicals. It also was the model for one of the most imitated plots in moviedom: The tyrant director, Warner Baxter, declaims the pep talk to end all pep talks to Ruby Keeler in a famous dressing room scene, ending with "Sawyer, you're going out a youngster but you've got to come back a star!" Ruby does her best, and darn if she doesn't bring the house down, despite some pretty clunky dancing. The elaborately staged Busby Berkeley numbers are highly entertaining, even after 60 years. A 1980 Broadway musical was based on the movie (and threw in another Harry Warren/Al Dubin song, "Lullaby of Broadway," from the movie *Gold Diggers of 1935*). Available on video.

THE GAY DIVORCEE

1934, RKO Radio Pictures

screenplay by George Marion Jr., Dorothy Yost, Edward Kaufman; produced by Pandro S. Berman; directed by Mark Sandrich; choreography by Dave Gould, Hermes Pan (Fred Astaire uncredited); photography by David Abel

major cast members: Fred Astaire, Ginger Rogers, Alice Brady, Edward Everett Horton, Erik Rhodes, Betty Grable, Lillian Miles, E.E. Clive

songs: Don't Let It Bother You (Harry Revel-Mack Gordon); A Needle in a Haystack (Con Conrad-Herb Magidson); Let's Knock K-nees (Revel-Gordon); Night and Day (Cole Porter); The Continental (Conrad-Magidson)

featured song in this collection: The Continental

The Hays office, the censorship authority that deemed what was acceptable for the movie-going public, didn't like the title of the 1932 Broadway musical *The Gay Divorce*, starring Fred Astaire. A divorce can't be gay, it decreed. As a result, the film version was renamed *The Gay Divorcee* when it was brought to the screen in 1934. The movie, about a married girl (Rogers) who travels to a seaside resort to get a divorce, really established the Astaire-Rogers formula for lighthearted comedy. The supporting cast, including Edward Everett Horton and Eric Blore, became part of the Astaire-Rogers "stock company." Erik Rhodes (retained from the stage

version) has a hilarious turn as a bumbling gigolo. The only song retained from Cole Porter's original score was "Night and Day," which became a classic dance duet for Astaire-Rogers. "The Continental" (written by Con Conrad and Herb Magidson) is a 17-minute showcase for the stars and an army of dancers, and became the first song to win an Oscar in the newly created best-song category. Available on video.

GIGI

1958, MGM

music by Frederick Loewe; lyrics & screenplay by Alan Jay Lerner; produced by Arthur Freed; directed by Vincente Minnelli (Charles Walters uncredited); photography by Joseph Ruttenberg

major cast members: Leslie Caron, Maurice Chevalier, Louis Jourdan, Hermione Gingold, Eva Gabor, Jacques Bergerac, Isabel Jeans, John Abbott, Monique Van Vooren

songs: Thank Heaven for Little Girls; The Parisians; It's a Bore; Gossip; She Is Not Thinking of Me; The Night They Invented Champagne; I Remember It Well; Gigi; I'm Glad I'm Not Young Anymore; Say a Prayer for Me Tonight

featured song in this collection: I Remember It Well

The curtain fell on the golden age of the MGM musical with Arthur Freed's spectacular production of Lerner & Loewe's original screen musical *Gigi*. For Freed, it was the crowning achievement on a remarkable career that began with *The Wizard of Oz* (he was associate producer) in 1939. Audrey Hepburn played *Gigi* in a 1954 non-musical Broadway production. For the musical, Freed cast Leslie Caron. Set in turn-of-the-century Paris, and adapted from a story by Collette, the story tells of a young French girl raised to be a courtesan who opts instead to marry. Louis Jourdan played the male romantic lead, and the part of his philandering uncle went to Maurice Chavalier. Most of the film was shot on location in Paris. For the sentimental "I Remember It Well,"

the location became a MGM sound stage, where against a painted backdrop, Gingold (as Gigi's grandmother) and Chevalier reminisce about their past love affair. When the Oscars were awarded *Gigi* became the most honored musical in history, winning nine awards, including best picture, best director (Vincente Minnelli), best song (the title tune) and an honorary award to Chevalier for his half-century contribution to the entertainment world. Available on video.

GOING MY WAY

1944, Paramount

music by James Van Heusen; lyrics by Johnny Burke; screenplay by Frank Butler & Frank Cavett; produced & directed by Leo McCarey; photography by Lionel Lindon

major cast members: Bing Crosby, Barry Fitzgerald, Risë Stevens, Frank McHugh, Jean Heather, Gene Lockhart, William Frawley, Stanley Clements, Carl Switzer, Adeline DeWalt Reynolds

songs: The Day After Forever; Silent Night (Franz Gruber); Too-Ra-Loo-Ra-Loo-Ral (J.B. Shannon); Habanera (Bizet); Going My Way; Ave Maria (Schubert); Swinging on a Star

featured song in this collection: Too-Ra-Loo-Ra-Loo-Ral

Any misgivings Bing Crosby may have had about going against type and playing a member of the clergy proved unfounded with the enormous success of *Going My Way*. In truth, it wasn't that much of a stretch for the popular crooner, who built his movie career around easy-going characters. The part of the Roman Catholic priest Father Chuck O'Malley was really no different. The film tells the story of a young priest (Crosby) who is dispatched by the archbishop to restore some order to St. Dominic's church, an ailing parish run by an aging and cantankerous head priest played by Barry Fitzgerald. Crosby sings the touching Irish lullaby "Too-Ra-Loo-Ra-Loo-Ral" to a bedridden Fitzgerald. The film concludes with Crosby strolling away from the church with the sweet strains of the song played in the background. *Going My Way* virtually swept the Academy Awards, winning Oscars for best picture, best actor (Crosby), best supporting actor (Fitzgerald), best director and original story (Leo McCarey) and best song ("Swinging On A Star"). Crosby made a sequel a year later, co-starring Ingrid Bergman, called *The Bells of St. Mary's*. Available on video.

THE HARVEY GIRLS

1946, MGM

music by Harry Warren; lyrics by Johnny Mercer; screenplay by Edmund Beloin, Nathaniel Curtis, Samson Raphaelson; produced by Arthur Freed; directed by George Sidney; choreography by Robert Alton; photography by George Folsey

major cast members: Judy Garland, John Hodiak, Ray Bolger, Angela Lansbury, Preston Foster, Virginia O'Brien, Kenny Baker, Cyd Charisse, Marjorie Main, Chill Wills, Selena Royle, Stephen McNally

songs: In the Valley Where the Evening Sun Goes Down; Wait and See; On the Atchison, Topeka and the Santa Fe; It's a Great Big World; The Wild, Wild West

featured song in this collection: On the Atchison, Topeka and the Santa Fe

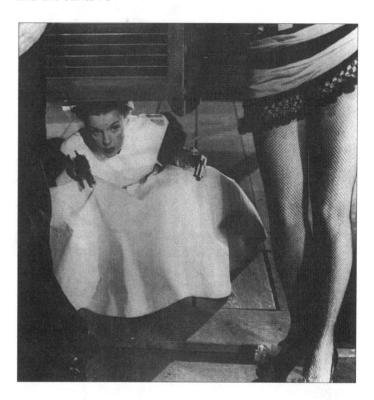

Following the unprecedented success of *Okahoma!* on Broadway, which opened in 1943, there were many nostalgic, period, rural musicals about the American west, and *The Harvey Girls* fits the bill. What, exactly, is a Harvey Girl? In the 1880s, businessman Fred Harvey began a chain of upstanding, moral, and wholesome restaurants along the train routes in the immoral and wild west, and recruited upstanding, moral and wholesome young women to work as waitresses. So we find Judy Garland, Virginia O'Brien, and their cohorts in a sorority of sorts, all hoping this adventure will lead to meeting Mr. Right. Across the street are the wicked charms of the saloon and its bevy of beauties, headed by Angela Lansbury (not even 20 when the movie was made, but already with an ageless worldliness). There are men to fight over, songs to sing, dances to dance, wisecracks to crack, and steaks and potatoes to serve. Judy gets her man in the end, and Angela is left appropriately alone and remorseful (this is the 40s, after all). There are some good songs, and one stand-out, the classic, huge number "On the Atchison, Topeka and the Santa Fe," where Judy and the whole town welcome the train. It's certainly one of the most exciting pieces of musical film from the 1940s. Available on video.

HIGH SOCIETY

1956, MGM

music & lyrics by Cole Porter; screenplay by John Patrick; produced by Sol C. Siegel; directed and choreography by Charles Walters; photography by Paul Vogel

major cast members: Bing Crosby, Grace Kelly, Frank Sinatra, Celeste Holm, John Lund, Louis Calhern, Sidney Blackmer, Louis Armstrong & band (Edmond Hall, Trummy Young, Billy Kyle, Arvell Shaw, Barrett Deems), Margalo Gilmore, Lydia Reed

songs: High Society Calypso, Little One, Who Wants to Be a Millionaire?; True Love; You're Sensational; I Love You, Samantha; Now You Has Jazz; Well, Did You Evah?; Mind If I Make Love to You?

featured song in this collection: True Love

High Society, Cole Porter's musical remake of playwright Philip Barry's 1939 stage hit *The Philadelphia Story*, contains two interesting musical footnotes. It was the first film pairing of singing legends Bing Crosby and Frank Sinatra, and it was Grace Kelly's final film before she left Hollywood to become Princess Grace of Monaco. Kelly plays a young society divorcee about to marry a stuffed-shirt (John Lund). Back into her life comes ex-husband Crosby, in town to help sponsor the Newport Jazz Festival (including visiting musician Louis Armstrong and his band), and convince Kelly that her marriage to Lund would be a mistake. Also entering the scene are *Spy* magazine reporter (Sinatra) and his photographer/girlfriend (Celeste Holm). After a good deal of pre-nuptial maneuvering, Crosby manages to win Kelly back. She receives a replica of their yacht as a wedding gift from Crosby, inspiring a flashback scene to their honeymoon aboard the boat (aptly named the True Love) where Crosby croons — what else — "True Love." Kelly joins in on the final verse and proves herself an adequate singer. Available on video.

* * * * * * * * * * * * * * * * * * * *

HIGH, WIDE AND HANDSOME

1937, Paramount

music by Jerome Kern; lyrics & screenplay by Oscar Hammerstein II; produced by Arthur Hornblow Jr.; directed by Rouben Mamoulian; choreography by LeRoy Prinz; photography by Victor Milner, Theodore Sparkuhl

major cast members: Irene Dunne, Randolph Scott, Dorothy Lamour, Raymond Walburn, Akim Tamiroff, Charles Bickford, Ben Blue, Elizabeth Patterson, William Frawley, Alan Hale, Lucien Littlefield, Rolfe Sedan

song: High, Wide and Handsome; Can I Forget you?; Will You Marry Me Tomorrow, Maria?; The Folks Who Live on the Hill; The Things I Want; Allegheny Al

featured song in this collection: The Folks Who Live on the Hill

The only original screen musical written by the songwriting team of Jerome Kern and Oscar Hammerstein II, *High, Wide and Handsome*, shares some similarities with their earlier stage success, *Show Boat*. Another slice of Americana, this romantic adventure recounts the newly discovered oil fields in western Pennsylvania in 1859 and follows the farmers' attempts to develop their find despite sabotage from a group of railroad money bosses (led by Alan Hale and Akim Tamiroff). The romantic interest is between Sally Waterson (Irene Dunne), a snake-oil salesman's daughter and idealistic farmer Peter Cortlandt (Randolph Scott). When the robber barons prevent Scott's men from laying a pipeline to the refinery, Dunne enlists her circus friends to help. The villains finally give up when they realize they're no match for a circus troupe, consisting of acrobats, sideshow freaks and elephants. Dunne's role is somewhat akin to her previous role of Magnolia Hawks in the 1936 film of *Show Boat*.

* * * * * * * * * * * * * * * * * * * *

HOLIDAY INN

1942, Paramount

music & lyrics by Irving Berlin; screenplay by Claude Binyon; produced and directed by Mark Sandrich; choreography by Danny Dare (Fred Astaire uncredited); photography by David Abel

major cast members: Bring Crosby, Fred Astaire, Marjorie Reynolds, Virginia Dale, Walter Abel, Louise Beavers, Harry Barris, Bob Crosby's Bob Cats, Leon Belasco, Marek Windheim, Irving Bacon, James Bell

songs: I'll Capture Your Heart Singing; Lazy; You're Easy to Dance With; White Christmas; Happy Holiday; Let's Start the New Year Right; Abraham; Be Careful, It's My Heart; I Can't Tell a Lie; Easter Parade; Song of Freedom; Let's Say It with Firecrackers; Plenty to Be Thankful For

featured song in this collection: I'll Capture Your Heart Singing

Holiday Inn was more than a name of a delightful screen entertainment starring Bing Crosby and Fred Astaire. The film inspired a hotel chain by the same name and introduced the mega-hit (and Oscar winner) "White Christmas." The plot finds Crosby playing an easy-going singer who abandons his dancing partner (Astaire) to live on a farm and escape the show business rat race. The good life turns into a nightmare, so he renovates the inn to operate as a nightclub on a holiday-only basis. This premise allowed Berlin to write nine songs for the eight featured holidays. Astaire plays a success-at-any-cost-cad and tries some unsavory tactics to steal Marjorie Reynolds away from Crosby as both his dance and romantic partner. "I'll Capture Your Heart singing" is a clever lyrical duel between Crosby and Astaire. In attempting to woo Virginia Dale, the two perform a challenge number: Crosby croons, Astaire taps, and each does a convincing imitation of the other. This film was followed four years later by another Crosby-Astaire-Berlin collaboration, *Blue Skies*. Available on video.

THE JAZZ SINGER

1927, Warner Brothers

screenplay by Alfred Cohen; titles by Jack Jarmuth; produced by Darryl F. Zanuck; directed by Alan Crosland; photography by Hal Mohr

major cast members: Al Jolson, May McAvoy, Warner Oland, Eugenie Besserer, Otto Lederer, Bobby Gordon, Roscoe Karns, Cantor Josef Rosenblatt, William Demarest, Myrna Loy

songs: Kol Nidre (traditional); Dirty Hands, Dirty Face (James Monaco-Edgar Leslie, Grant Clarke); Toot, Toot Tootsie! (Ted Fiorito, Robert King-Gus Kahn); Yahrzeit (traditional); Blue Skies (Irving Berlin); Mother of Mine, I Still Have You (Louis Silvers-Clarke); My Mammy (Walter Donaldson-Sam Lewis, Joe Young)

featured song in this collection: My Mammy

The first full-length "talkie" (actually it was only partially sound), *The Jazz Singer* also had the distinction of being the first screen musical. The immense success of the film meant sound was not a fad as predicted by rival studio moguls. The movie was based on a 1925 stage show, which starred George Jessel. Tapped to recreate the role as Jakie Rabinowitz, the cantor's son who upsets his parents by leaving home to become a jazz singer by the name of Jack Robin, Jessel withdrew when Warner Brothers did not meet his salary demands. In stepped vaudeville legend Al Jolson and with the words, "Wait a minute! Wait a minute! You ain't heard nothin' yet…" history was made. In a departure from the stage production, the film ends with the black-faced Jolson belting out "My Mammy" to his beaming mother in the audience at a Broadway revue. The film was

remade twice, first with Danny Thomas in 1952 and in 1980 starring Neil Diamond. Available on video.

KISS ME KATE

1953, MGM

music & lyrics by Cole Porter; screenplay by Dorothy Kingsley; produced by Jack Cummings; directed by George Sidney; choreography by Hermes Pan (Bob Fosse uncredited); photography by Charles Rosher

major cast members: Kathryn Grayson, Howard Keel, Ann Miller, Tommy Rall, Keenan Wynn, James Whitmore, Bobby Van, Bob Fosse, Kurt Kaszner, Ron Randell, Williard Parker, Carol Haney, Jeanne Coyne, Claud Allister, Dave O'Brien

songs: So in Love; Too Darn Hot; Why Can't You Behave?; Wunderbar; We Open in Venice; Tom, Dick, or Harry; I've Come to Wive It Wealthily in Padua; I Hate Men; Were Thine That Special Face; Where Is the Life That Late I Led?; Always True to You (in My Fashion); Brush Up Your Shakespeare; From This Moment On

featured song in this collection: Too Darn Hot

Of his eight Broadway musicals, Cole Porter's *Kiss Me, Kate* was his greatest success (with a comma on Broadway, without in Hollywood). The story was inspired by Shakespeare's *The Taming of the Shrew*. *Kiss Me, Kate* is a play within a play. The backstage story involves two thespians (and former husband and wife), played on film by Howard Keel and Kathryn Grayson. The second story is the musical retelling of the Shakespeare comedy. When Keel reveals a casual interest in the show's co-star (Ann Miller), it causes Grayson to play the shrew both on and off-stage. Choreographer Hermes Pan used his stellar cast of dancers, including Miller, Bob Fosse, Bobby Van, Tommy Rall and Carol Haney, to full advantage. The result is a series of electrifying dances. In the number, "Too Darn Hot," Ann Miller, (bedecked in an appropriately red sequined dress) demonstrates why she was MGM's "queen of tap." The number sizzles with her rapid-fire tapping. *Kiss Me Kate* was the only musical ever filmed in 3D – a short-lived fad that was used in an attempt to compete with the growing popularity of television. That explains why cast members are regularly throwing props at the camera. Available on video.

LES GIRLS

1957, MGM

music and lyrics by Cole Porter; screenplay by John Patrick; produced by Sol C. Siegel; directed by George Cukor; choreography by Jack Cole (Gene Kelly uncredited); photography by Robert Surtees

major cast members: Gene Kelly, Mitzi Gaynor, Kay Kendall, Taina Elg, Jacques Bergerac, Henry Daniell, Patrick Macnee, Leslie Phillips

songs: Les Girls; Ca C'est L'Amour; Ladies in Waiting; You're Just Too, Too!; Why Am I So Gone About That Gal?"

featured song in this collection: You're Just Too, Too!

For Gene Kelly, *Les Girls* ended a 15-year association (and 18 films) with MGM. For Cole Porter the film marked his last original motion picture score. *Les Girls* is a musical comedy about a libel suit with plot similarities taken from the Japanese classic *Rashoman*. Kelly is an American entertainer with an international act consisting of "Les Girls," a scatterbrained Briton (Kay Kendall), a French beauty (Finnish ballerina Taina Elg) and a level-headed American (Mitzi Gaynor). The courtroom scene recalls differing testimony of the perceived truth and serves as the background for flashbacks featuring Kelly, his ladies and the act. The suit attempts to uncover what really happened kin Paris in 1949 between Kelly and his girls. The film uses humor to relate

three tales from three different viewpoints. Famed "woman's director" George Cukor kept the film moving at a lively pace. Cole Porter's jabbing of the upper crust is delightfully performed by Kelly and Kendall in the energetic "You're Just Too, Too!" Available on video.

LOVE ME OR LEAVE ME

1955, MGM

screenplay by Daniel Fuchs & Isobel Lennart; produced by Joe Pasternak; directed by Charles Vidor; choreography by Alex Romero; photography by Arthur Arling

major cast members: James Cagney, Doris Day, Cameron Mitchell, Robert Keith, Tom Tully, Claude Stroud, Harry Bellaver, Richard Gaines, Joe Pasternak

songs: It All Depends on You (Ray Henderson-B.G. DeSylva, Lew Brown); You Made Me Love You (James Monaco-Joe McCarthy); Everybody Loves My Baby (Spencer Williams-Jack Palmer); Sam the Old Accordion Man (Walter Donaldson); Shaking the Blues Away (Irving Berlin); Ten Cents a Dance (Richard Rodgers-Lorenz Hart); I'll Never Stop Loving You (Nicholas Brodszky-Sammy Cahn); At Sundown (Donaldson); Love Me or Leave Me (Donaldson-Gus Kahn)

featured song in this collection: Love Me or Leave Me

Love Me or Leave Me is a refreshing change from some of the more sugar-coated film biographies that Hollywood produced. In this case, the subject is torch singer Ruth Etting (played effectively by Doris Day) and her torrid affair and marriage with racketeer Marty "The Gimp" Snyder (vividly portrayed by James Cagney). With appropriate strong arm tactics, Snyder elevates Etting to major star status. Caught in the emotional roller coaster is Etting's accompanist (Cameron Mitchell), who even takes a bullet from the ever-jealous Cagney. The score includes about a dozen songs written during Etting's era plus two new songs. Day's performance packs an emotional wallop and her vocals invoke a true torch singer's quality, including the powerful title song. In his autobiography, Cagney said the film proved Day to be an exceptional talent and called her roles in such lightweight entertainments as *Pillow Talk* "one hell of a waste." Available on video.

LOVE ME TONIGHT

1932, Paramount

music by Richard Rodgers, lyrics by Lorenz Hart; screenplay by Samuel Hoffenstein, Waldemar Young, George Marion Jr.; produced and directed by Rouben Mamoulian; photography by Victor Milner

major cast members: Maurice Chevalier, Jeanette MacDonald, Charlie Ruggles, Charles Butterworth, Myrna Loy, C. Aubrey Smith, Elizabeth Patterson, Ethel Griffies, Blance Friderici, Joseph Cawthorn, Robert Greig, Bert Roach, George "Gabby" Hayes, Tyler Brooke, Herbert Mundin, Cecil Cunningham, Marion "Peanuts" Byron, Rolfe Sedan, Edgar Norton, Rita Owin, Mel Calish

songs: That's the Song of Paree; Isn't It Romantic?; Lover; Mimi; A Woman Needs Something Like That; The Deer Hunt (instrumental); The Poor Apache; Love Me Tonight; The Son of a Gun Is Nothing but a Tailor

featured song in this collection: Isn't It Romantic?

Before Jeanette McDonald formed her legendary screen partnership with Nelson Eddy, she co-starred with Maurice Chevalier in the musical classic *Love Me Tonight*. Famed director Rouben Mamoulian took an uncompleted play by Leopold Marchand and Paul Arment and turned it into one of the first integrated musicals, where the songs provided a natural progression for the plot. An example is the use of the song, "Isn't It Romantic?" which moves the story from Chevalier's tailor shop to McDonald's chateau in the French countryside. Chevalier plays a carefree Parisian tailor who travels to a countryside castle to collect a debt from Vicomte

de Vareze (Charlie Ruggles). Enroute he encounters Princess Jeanette (McDonald), who coincidentally also lives at the chateau. To save face, and protect his standing with the Duke (C. Aubrey Smith), Ruggles introduces Chevalier as a baron to the castle inhabitants. Nobility has its privileges and McDonald takes a liking to him. When the hoax is discovered, she first rejects him, but then decides to go forth in romantic pursuit.

MARY POPPINS

1964, Walt Disney

music & lyrics by Richard Sherman & Robert Sherman; screenplay by Bill Walsh & Donald Da Gradi; produced by Walt Disney; directed by Robert Stevenson; choreography by Marc Breaux & DeeDee Wood; photography by Edward Colman

major cast members: Julie Andrews, Dick Van Dyke, David Tomlinson, Glynis Johns, Ed Wynn, Hermione Baddeley, Karen Dotrice, Matthew Garber, Elsa Lanchester, Arthur Treacher, Reginald Owen, Reta Shaw, Jane Darwell

songs: Chim Chim Cheree; Sister Suffragette; The Life I Lead; A Spoonful of Sugar, Jolly Holiday; I Love to Laugh; Supercalifragilisticexpialidocious; Stay Awake; Feed the Birds; Step in Time; Let's Go Fly a Kite

featured song in this collection: Feed the Birds

Julie Andrews may have been passed over for the lead in *My Fair Lady* (she originated the role of Eliza Doolittle in the 1956 stage production), but she still made an auspicious film debut in *Mary Poppins*. In fact she picked up an Academy Award for best actress. Her *My Fair Lady* replacement, Audrey Hepburn, (considered a safer box office bet at the time) was not even nominated. The film is based on the Pamela Travers' children's classic, set in turn-of-the-century London. Andrews, in the title role, plays a whimsical nanny who comes down from the clouds (literally) to care for two young children. Travers forbid Disney from linking the Poppins character romantically with Bert (Dick Van Dyke), the likable one-man band and chalk artist, whom Andrews and the children meet in the park. Also true to the original, Mary Poppins leaves the Banks family in the same way she arrived, by umbrella. The score for the musical fantasy included the Oscar-winner "Chim Chim Cheree." Andrew's would continue to perfect her nanny role in her next screen assignment, *The Sound of Music*. Available on video.

MEET ME IN ST. LOUIS
1944, MGM

music & lyrics by Hugh Martin & Ralph Blane; screenplay by Irving Brecher, Fred Finklehoffe; produced by Arthur Freed; directed by Vincente Minnelli; choreography by Charles Walters; photography by George Folsey

major cast members: Judy Garland, Margaret O'Brien, Mary Astor, Lucille Bremer, Leon Ames, Tom Drake, Marjorie Main, Harry Davenport, June Lockhart, Hugh Marlowe, Chill Wills, Darryl Hickman, Joan Carroll, Henry Daniels Jr.

songs: Meet Me in St. Louis, Louis (Kerry Mills-Andrew Sterling); The Boy Next Door; Under the Bamboo Tree (J. Rosamond Johnson-Bob Cole); The Trolley Song; You and I (Nacio Herb Brown, Arthur Freed); Have Yourself a Merry Little Christmas

featured song in this collection: Under the Bamboo Tree

Few movie musicals have attained the classic status of *Meet Me in St. Louis*. Although some studio executives balked at the idea of making a film that was essentially void of plot, action and conflict, producer Arthur Freed prevailed. He knew the nostalgic, sentimental story of the Smith family, based on a series of short stories by Sally Benson, would make a memorable musical. The story takes place in St. Louis during a year-long period leading up to the 1904 World's Fair. The film follows the lives and loves of the family and the crisis that is nearly caused when the patriarch (Leon Ames) announces that the brood is moving to New York.

Although Judy Garland, as the second oldest Smith daughter, was the star, it was really an ensemble film. Hugh Martin and Ralph Blane were given their first songwriting assignment at MGM. The team delivered with "The Boy Next Door," "The Trolley Song" and "Have Yourself a Merry Little Christmas." The score also included period pieces such as "Under the Bamboo Tree," which is performed as a cakewalk by Garland and her precocious 5 year old sister, played by Margaret O'Brien. Available on video.

MISSISSIPPI
1935, Paramount

music by Richard Rodgers; lyrics by Lorenz Hart; screenplay by Francis Martin & Jack Cunningham; produced by Arthur Hornblow; directed by A. Edward Sutherland; photography by Charles Lang

major cast members: Bing Crosby, W.C. Fields, Joan Bennett, Queenie Smith, Gail Patrick, Claude Gillingwater, John Miljan, Ann Sheridan, Dennis O'Keefe, King Baggott, Paul Hurst

songs: Roll Mississippi; Soon; Down by the River; It's Easy to Remember; Old Folks at Home (Stephen Foster)

featured song in this collection: It's Easy to Remember

Considered more a comedy than a musical *Mississippi* teamed the nation's most popular crooner, Bing Crosby, with legendary film comic W.C. Fields. An adaptation of Booth Tarkington's 1923 play, *Magnolia*, the movie tells the story of a meek young man (Crosby) who is disgraced when he loses honor by refusing take part in a duel for the hand of his fiancé (Gail Patrick). Humiliated, Crosby becomes an entertainer on a theatrical river boat run by Fields. When things get a bit unruly during a performance, Crosby regains his honor by duking it out with a villainous river rat (Fred Kohler). Fields exploits Crosby's new-found machismo by billing him as the Singing Killer. Replete with a mustache and mutton chops, the fisticuffs scene was somewhat of a departure for the easy-going Crosby. Crosby wins the affections of Patrick's younger sister (Joan Bennett). With the score completed, Crosby requested another song from composers Rodgers and Hart. They delivered with the hit, "It's Easy to Remember."

MY FAIR LADY

1964, Warner Brothers

music by Frederick Loewe; lyrics & screenplay by Alan Jay Lerner; produced by Jack L. Warner; directed by George Cukor; choreography by Hermes Pan, photography by Harry Stradling

major cast members: Audrey Hepburn, Rex Harrison, Stanley Holloway, Wilfred Hyde-White, Gladys Cooper, Jeremy Brett, Theodore Bikel, Mona Washbourne, Isobel Elsom, Henry Daniell, Grady Sutton, Charles Fredericks, John Holland, Owen McGiveney, Lily Kemble Cooper, Moyna MacGill, Olive Reeves-Smith, Barbara Pepper, Baroness Bina Rothschild

songs: Why Can't the English?; Wouldn't It Be Lovely?; I'm an Ordinary Man; With a Little Bit of Luck; Just You Wait; The Rain in Spain; I Could Have Danced All Night; Ascot Gavotte; On the Street Where You Live; Embassy Waltz (instrumental); You Did It; Show Me; Get Me to the Church on Time; A Hymn to Him; Without You; I've Grown Accustomed to Her Face

featured song in this collection: I've Grown Accustomed to Her Face

It took eight years before Alan Jay Lerner and Frederick Loewe brought their stage hit, *My Fair Lady* to the screen. The coveted part of Eliza Doolittle, the girl that undergoes a transformation from the wistful cockney refined lady did not go to the show's Broadway lead, Julie Andrews. Instead, Jack Warner went with established screen star Audrey Hepburn (her vocals were dubbed by Marni Nixon). When Cary Grant turned down the male lead of Professor Henry Higgins and James Cagney couldn't be wooed out of retirement to play Alfred Doolittle, Warner cast the Broadway originals, Rex Harrison and Stanley Holloway, respectively. Lerner's screenplay assured that the film adaptation was faithful to the stage script, which was based on George Bernard Shaw's 1914 play *Pygmalion*. In a departure from the original Shaw work, the interminable bachelor Harrison falls in love with his pupil-turned-princess. He grudgingly admits his affections for Eliza by singing "I've Grown Accustomed To Her Face." The film won several Oscars, including best picture, best actor (Harrison) and best director (George Cukor). Available on video.

● ● ● ● ● ● ● ● ● ● ● ● ● ● ● ●

NAUGHTY MARIETTA

1935, MGM

music by Victor Herbert; lyrics by Rida Johnson Young; screenplay by John Lee Mahin, Frances Goodrich, Albert Hackett; produced by Hunt Stromberg; directed by W.S. Van Dyke; photography by William Daniels

major cast members: Jeanette MacDonald; Nelson Eddy, Frank Morgan, Elsa Lanchester, Douglass Dumbrille, Joseph Cawthorn, Cecilia Parker, Akim Tamiroff, Edward Brophy, Marjorie Main, Walter Kingsford

songs: Chansonette (lyric: Gus Kahn); Tramp, Tramp, Tramp; 'Neath the Southern Moon; Italian Street Song; I'm Falling in Love With Someone; Ah! Sweet Mystery of Life

featured song in this collection: Ah! Sweet Mystery of Life

If Fred Astaire and Ginger Rogers were America's dancing sweethearts, the title of singing sweethearts had to be bestowed on Nelson Eddy and Jeanette MacDonald. The team co-starred in eight operettas together. The first was Victor Herbert's *Naughty Marietta*. Based on the 1910 stage show, the story of a French noblewoman (MacDonald) who leaves her homeland to avoid a loveless marriage and meets up with a backwoods soldier of fortune (Eddy) in 17th century New Orleans, was the perfect vehicle for the pair. The film had it all: the spectacle of MacDonald's departure from France, swashbuckling action, a nasty villain (Douglass Dumbrille), decent comic relief (Frank Morgan and Elsa Lanchester), and of course, the love story provided by the two stars. It's a love that's consummated when the two miraculously find the words to "Ah! Sweet Mystery of Life." (The song once again made it to the screen, this time sung by Madeleine Kahn in the 1974 Mel Brooks film *Young Frankenstein*.) Available on video.

OKLAHOMA!

1955, Magna

music by Ricard Rodgers; lyrics by Oscar Hammerstein II; screenplay by Sonya Levien, William Ludwig; produced by Arthur Hornblow Jr.; directed by Fred Zinnemann; choreography by Agnes de Mille; photography by Robert Surtees

major cast members: Gordon MacRae, Gloria Grahame, Shirley Jones, Charlotte Greenwood, Eddie Albert, Gene Nelson, James Whitmore, Rod Steiger, Jay C. Flippen, Marc Platt, James Mitchell, Bambi Linn, Kelly Brown, Barbara Lawrence

songs: Oh, What a Beautiful Mornin'; The Surrey With the Fringe on Top; Kansas City; I Cain't Say No; Many a New Day; People Will Say We're in Love; Pore Jud; Out of My Dreams; The Farmer and the Cowman; All er Nothin'; Oklahoma

featured song in this collection: People Will Say We're in Love

It took 12 years to bring the long-running Broadway classic *Oklahoma!* to the screen. The show, based on a 1931 play by Lynn Riggs, *Green Grow the Lilacs*, was a landmark in it's day, due primarily to its unforgettable score and integration of story, music and dance. The producers refused a movie deal until the show had finished its Broadway run and national tours. With the advent of the widescreen process called Todd-AO, composers Richard Rodgers and Oscar Hammerstein II felt the scope of their work could be given the appropriate screen treatment. The story of the ranch hand Curly (Gordon MacRae) and his courtship with farmgirl Laurey Williams (Shirley Jones), remained faithful to the original. The distinctive choreography by Agnes de Mille was also retained. The supporting cast was excellent, including Rod Steiger as the menacing farmhand Jud Fry, Charlotte Greenwood as Laurey's Aunt Eller, Gene Nelson as the likeable rancher Will Parker, Gloria Grahame as the flirtatious Ado Annie and Eddie Albert as the Persian peddler Ali Hakim. For famed director Fred Zinnemann, it was his first musical assignment, although he had some experience with cowboys — a few years earlier he directed the classic, *High Noon*. As the romance between MacRae and Jones blossoms, the two sing the duet "People Will Say We're in Love." Available on video.

ON THE TOWN

1949, MGM

music by Leonard Bernstein, Roger Edens; lyrics & screenplay by Betty Comden, Adolph Green; produced by Arthur Freed; directed & choreography by Gene Kelly, Stanley Donen; photography by Harold Rosson

major cast members: Gene Kelly, Frank Sinatra, Betty Garrett, Ann Miller, Jules Munshin, Vera-Ellen, Florence Bates, Alice Pearce, Hans Conreid, Carol Haney, George Meader, Bea Benaderet

songs: I Feel Like I'm Not Out of Bed Yet; New York, New York; Miss Turnstiles ballet (instrumental); Prehistoric Man; Come Up to My Place; Main Street; You're Awful; On the Town; Count on Me; A Day in New York ballet (instrumental)

featured song in this collection: New York, New York

On the Town was the first film to shoot a musical number on location. It was a logistical nightmare for cast and crew, but it was worth it. The film's highlight remains the opening sequence, "New York, New York," in which three sailors (Gene Kelly, Frank Sinatra and Jules Munshin) cavort at various Big Apple landmarks. The original lyric to the song, "New York, New York — it's a helluva town" was deemed unacceptable by the film censors and was replaced with the words "it's a wonderful town." Producer Arthur Freed never thought much of the otherwise acclaimed Leonard Bernstein, Betty Comden and Adolph Green score (from the original 1944 Broadway musical), so only two songs and two ballets were retained. The rest of the score was written by Roger Edens and Comden and Green. The story of three sailors on 24-hour shore leave in New York who find romance with three girls (Ann Miller, Vera-Ellen and Betty Garrett) remained relatively faithful to the stage version. The film was the first co-directorial assignment for Gene Kelly and Stanley Donen, who went on to co-direct *Singin' in the Rain* and *It's Always Fair Weather*. Available on video.

PAL JOEY
1957, Columbia

music by Richard Rodgers; lyrics by Lorenz Hart; screenplay by Dorothy Kingsley; produced by Fred Kohlmar; directed by George Sidney; choreography by Hermes Pan; photography by Harold Lipstein

major cast members: Rita Hayworth, Frank Sinatra, Kim Novak, Barbara Nichols, Bobby Sherwood, Hank Henry, Elizabeth Patterson, Hermes Pan

songs: That Terrific Rainbow; I Didn't Know What Time it Was; Great Big Town; There's a Small Hotel; Zip; I Could Write a Book; The Lady Is a Tramp; Bewitched; My Funny Valentine

featured song in this collection: I Could Write a Book

Gene Kelly originated the part of the dancing cad Joey Evans in the 1940 Broadway musical *Pal Joey*. Columbia studio chief Harry Cohn bought the property with the intent of reuniting Kelly with his *Cover Girl* co-star Rita Hayworth. MGM, the actor's studio, refused to lend Kelly to Columbia. Consequently, Cohn waited until 1957 to finally make "Joey" with Frank Sinatra in the title role. Cohn also indulged himself by casting his own "love goddesses," Rita Hayworth and Kim Novak. In addition to changing Joey's occupation from dancing cad to singing cad, the film version also switched the locale from Chicago to San Francisco, and the vocations of Hayworth and Novak. Of the 14 original Rodgers and Hart songs, eight were retained (two as instrumental pieces) and four numbers were added from their other shows. With Nelson Riddle's orchestrations, and the classic Rodgers and Hart tunes, including "I Could Write a Book," Sinatra was at his vocal prime. Available on video.

THE PIRATE
1948 MGM

words & music by Cole Porter; screenplay by Frances Goodrich & Albert Hackett; produced by Arthur Freed, directed by Vincente Minnelli; choreography by Robert Alton, Gene Kelly; photography by Harry Stradling

major cast members: Judy Garland, Gene Kelly, Walter Slezak, Gladys Cooper, Reginald Owen, Nicholas Brothers, George Zucco, Lester Allen, Cully Richards, Lola Albright,

Jerry Bergen, Ben Lessy, Lola Deem, Ellen Ross, Mary Jo Ellis

songs: Niña; Mack the Black; You Can Do No Wrong; Be a Clown; Love of My Life

featured song in this collection: Be a Clown

The Pirate, a big, colorful musical, had all the ingredients for success: a winning Cole Porter score, crisp direction by Vincente Minnelli and top notch performances from stars Judy Garland (Minnelli's wife at the time) and Gene Kelly. When the film was released, it laid an egg. Critics loved it, but audiences turned away. Perhaps the 19th century story of a convent-reared girl (Judy Garland) and her fantasies of the notorious pirate Macoco was too sophisticated for post-World War II audiences. Kelly plays a traveling actor who learns of Garland's dreams of her pirate hero and claims to be the infamous Macoco. The whole situation gets messed up when Garland's fiancé, the overweight and lazy mayor of the village (Walter Slezak) reveals himself to be the actual pirate. The film was already in production when Kelly urged Porter to write a boisterous clown song for Garland and himself. The result, "Be a Clown" — a dance performed by Kelly and the electrifying Nicholas Brothers. The song is reprised at the end of the film by Garland and Kelly, replete with rubber noses and baggy pants. Available on video.

ROBERTA
1935 RKO Radio Pictures

music by Jerome Kern; lyrics by Otto Harbach, Dorothy Fields; screenplay by Jane Murfin, Sam Mintz, Glen Tryon, Allan Scott; produced by Pandro S. Berman; directed by William Seiter; choreography by Hermes Pan (Fred Astaire uncredited); photography by Edward Cronjager

major cast members: Irene Dunne, Fred Astaire, Ginger Rogers, Randolph Scott, Helen Westley, Victor Varconi, Claire Dodd, Lucille Ball, Candy Candido, Gene Sheldon

songs: Let's Begin (lyric: Fields); I'll Be Hard to Handle (lyric: Bernard Dougall); Yesterdays (lyric: Harbach); I Won't Dance; (lyric with Oscar Hammerstein II); Smoke Gets in Your Eyes (lyric: Harbach); Lovely to Look At (lyric: Fields)

featured song in this collection: Smoke Gets in Your Eyes

Roberta was the third film to team Fred Astaire and Ginger Rogers. And like its predecessor, *The Gay Divorcee*, it too was adapted from a Broadway musical. The 1933 stage show is best remembered as the play that catapulted a young comedian by the name of Bob Hope to stardom and introduced the classic Jerome Kern song "Smoke Gets in Your Eyes." RKO used the film to showcase its hot new dance team (Astaire and Rogers) as well as its only other bonafide star, Irene Dunne, who was paired with Randolph Scott. In the film, a former football player (Scott) inherits his aunt's Parisian dress salon (named Roberta) and becomes romantically involved with her assistant, an exiled Russian princess (Dunne). The Astaire-Rogers romance is secondary (and almost non-existent), but it's enough to create some memorable moments on the dance floor, including the climactic end of "Smoke Gets in Your Eyes," where they swing themselves onto a stairway. From the original stage production, four Kern tunes were dropped and two new ones were added: "Lovely to Look At" and "I Won't Dance." Available on video.

ROSALIE

1937, MGM

music & lyrics by Cole Porter; screenplay & produced by William Anthony McGuire; directed by W.S. Van Dyke; choreography by Albertina Rasch; photography by Oliver Marsh

major cast members: Nelson Eddy, Eleanor Powell, Ray Bolger, Frank Morgan, Ilona Massey, Edma May Oliver, Billy Gilbert, Reginald Owen, George Zucco, Virginia Grey, William Demarest, Jerry Colonna, Al Shean, Janet Beecher, Pierre Watkin

songs: Who Knows?; I've a Strange New Rhythm in My Heart; Rosalie; In the Still of the Night; Spring Love Is in the Air

featured song in this collection: Rosalie

Rosalie took Nelson Eddy away from Jeanette MacDonald and teamed him with MGM's tap dancing star Eleanor Powell. This lavish production shares the same story as a 1928 stage production, but the entire score was scrapped in favor of a new one by Cole Porter. An Army-Navy football game is the unlikely setting where cadet Dick Thorpe (Eddy) wins the game much to the admiration of Rosalie (Powell), the princess of Romanza, who is enrolled incognito at Vassar. An arranged marriage for the princess takes our lovelorn stars back to Romanza and then back again to the U.S. Although Porter didn't think much of his title song,

MGM studio chief Louis B. Mayer personally requested the tune sound as close as possible to "Rose Marie" (the title song of an earlier Eddy-MacDonald film). MacDonald was in disfavor with Mayer at the time and this was seen as a retaliatory measure on his part. In an elaborate production number (the film cost approximately $2 million), Powell, Eddy and a cast of thousands, sing and dance the title tune. Available on video.

SAN FRANCISCO

1936, MGM

music & lyrics by various writers; screenplay by Anita Loos, Robert Hopkins; produced by John Emerson, Bernard Hyman; directed by W. S. Van Dyke; choreography by Val Raset; photography by Oliver T. Marsh

major cast members: Jeanette MacDonald, Clark Gable, Spencer Tracy, Jack Holt, Ted Healy, Jessie Ralph, Margaret Irving, Shirley Ross, Al Shean

songs, arias: San Francisco (Bronislau Kpaer/Gus Kahn), A Heart That's Free (Alfred Robyn/T. Reilley), Would You? (Nacio Herb Brown/Arthur Freed), Sempre libera from *La Traviata* (Verdi), Jewel Song from *Faust* (Gounod)

featured song in this collection: San Francisco

Set in 1906, the movie is a musicalized rendering of the great earthquake that rocked San Francisco, possibly the first true disaster movie. The box-office results were hardly a disaster though. *San Francisco* was one of the top-grossing movies of its time. Jeanette MacDonald plays a singer who divides her time between a café act and the opera. Gable plays the cabaret owner in love with MacDonald. For the movie's last 20 minutes the earth moves and shakes. Though melodramatic, this movie is exciting and moving, and shows both MacDonald and Gable at their best. Available on video.

SHALL WE DANCE

1937, RKO Radio Pictures

music by George Gershwin; lyrics by Ira Gershwin; screenplay by Allan Scott & Ernest Pagano; produced by Pandro S. Berman; directed by Mark Sandrich; choreography by Hermes Pan, Harry Losee (Fred Astaire uncredited); photography by David Abel

major cast members: Fred Astaire, Ginger Rogers, Edward Everett Horton, Eric Blore, Jerome Cowan, Ketti Gallian, Harriet Hoctor, Ann Shoemaker, Ben Alexander, William Brisbane, Marek Windheim, Rolfe Sedan, Emma Young

songs: (I've Got) Beginner's Luck; Slap That Bass; Walking the Dog (instrumental); They All Laughed; Let's Call the Whole Thing Off; They Can't Take That Away from Me; Shall We Dance

featured song in this collection: Let's Call the Whole Thing Off

After Jerome Kern, Irving Berlin (twice) and Cole Porter, it was now George and Ira Gershwin's turn to write the score for a Fred Astaire-Ginger Rogers movie. Their seventh screen pairing, *Shall We Dance*, follows the tried and true Astaire-Rogers formula involving mistaken identity. Astaire plays Pete Peters, as American dancer, who goes by the name Petrov. While in Paris, he becomes obsessed with another American entertainer (Rogers). The two have plenty of time to nurture the romance on a New York-bound ocean liner. More complications and plot twists develop stateside, but by film's end the two reunite during a production number that finds all the chorus girls wearing masks of Rogers. The Gershwins' score produced three song standards, including the lyrical duel over proper pronunciation, "Let's Call the Whole Thing Off." The vocal was followed by a roller skate routine around Central Park by Astaire and Rogers, a number that took four days to shoot. After *Shall We Dance* was released in April of 1937, it would be a year and a half before another movie featuring the famous pair would be released. In the meantime, Astaire and Rogers each made films on their own. Available on video.

SHOW BOAT

1951, MGM

music by Jerome Kern; lyrics by Oscar Hammerstein II; screenplay by John Lee Mahin; produced by Arthur Freed, directed by George Sidney; choreography by Robert Alton; photography by Charles Rosher

major cast members: Kathryn Grayson, Ava Gardner, Howard Keel, Joe E. Brown, Marge & Gower Champion, Robert Sterling, Agnes Moorehead, Leif Erickson, William Warfield, Regis Toomey, Fuzzy Knight, Chick Chandler,

songs: Make Believe; Can't Help Lovin' Dat Man; I Might Fall Back on You; Ol' Man River; You Are Love; Why Do I Love You?; Bill (lyric with P.G. Wodehouse); Life Upon the Wicked Stage; After the Ball (Charles K. Harris)

featured song in this collection: Make Believe

SILK STOCKINGS

1957, MGM

music & lyrics by Cole Porter; screenplay by Leonard Gershe & Leonard Spigelgass (Harry Kurnitz uncredited); produced by Arthur Freed; directed by Rouben Mamoulian; choreography by Eugene Loring, Hermes Pan (Fred Astaire uncredited); photography by Robert Bronner

major cast members: Fred Astaire, Cyd Charisse, Janis Paige, Peter Lorre, Jules Munshin, George Tobias, Joseph Buloff, Wim Sonneveld, Barrie Chase, Belita, Tybee Afra, Betty Uitti, Kaaren Verne, Rolfe Sedan, Eugene Borden

songs: Too Bad; Paris Loves Lovers; Stereophonic Sound; It's a Chemical Reaction, That's All; All of You; Satin and Silk; Without Love; Fated to Be Mated; Josephine; Siberia; The Red Blues; The Ritz Roll and Rock

featured song in this collection: All of You

Director George Sidney said in an interview, "the only reason to remake a film is if the original was lousy." He was undoubtedly referring to the 1936 production of the 1936 Jerome Kern-Oscar Hammerstein II musical **Show Boat**, starring Irene Dunne and Allan (father of Jack) Jones, although that screen rendition has plenty of defenders. Sidney's 1951 technicolor remake was one of the biggest money-makers of all MGM musicals. Based on the Edna Ferber novel, *Show Boat* first appeared as a Broadway musical in 1927. Sidney's film adaptation paired Howard Keel and Kathryn Grayson, who went on to make two more films together. The plot presents two love stories — one between riverboat gambler Gaylord Ravenal (Keel) and Magnolia Hawks (Grayson), daughter of the showboat captain (Joe E. Brown), the other, considered bold in its day, concerned the inter-racial marriage between mulatto actress Julie La Verne (Ava Gardner), and her white leading man (Robert Sterling). The Kern-Hammerstein score is full of melodic standards, including "Make Believe," sung as a duet by Keel and Grayson after their initial meeting on the deck of the paddle wheeler. The vocal highlight remains William Warfield's moving rendition of "Ol' Man River." Available on video.

● ● ● ● ● ● ● ● ● ● ● ● ● ● ●

Poking fun at Communism may seem a bit dated today. But in 1939 it was quite in vogue. That was the year Greta Garbo's *Ninotchka* was released to much acclaim. The story about a female Russian agent captivated by Paris and all its capitalistic trappings became the basis for Cole Porter's last Broadway musical in 1955, the thick of the cold war, renamed *Silk Stockings*. In 1957, producer Arthur Freed brought it to the screen in an exuberant Cinemascope production. To accommodate stars Fred Astaire and Cyd Charisse, a heavier emphasis was placed on the dancing, but the basic story remained the same: Ninotchka is dispatched to Paris to return three AWOL Russian agents (Jules Munshin, Joseph Buloff and Peter Lorre). While on her mission she slowly falls under the hypnotic spell of American film maker (Astaire) and eventually abandons "Mother Russia." Astaire begins to melt the Russian's heart when he sings of "All of You" (the lyrics caused quite a stir at the time). Porter's ode to rock n' roll, "The Ritz Roll and Rock" was Astaire's last on-screen opportunity to dance in top hat, white tie and tails (not counting Astaire's hosting chores in the 1976 film, *That's Entertainment Part II*). Available on video.

SINGIN' IN THE RAIN

1952, MGM

music by Nacio Herb Brown; lyrics by Arthur Freed; screenplay by Betty Comden, Adolph Green; produced by Arthur Freed; directed/choreograhed by Gene Kelly, Stanley Donen; photography by Harold Rosson

major cast members: Gene Kelly, Donald O'Connor, Debbie Reynolds, Jean Hagen, Millard Mitchell, Cyd Charisse, Rita Moreno, Jimmy Thompson

songs: Singin' in the Rain; Fit as a Fiddle (Al Hoffman/Al Goodhart); All I Do Is Dream of You; Make 'Em Laugh; I've Got a Feelin' You're Foolin'; Should I?; Beautiful Girl; You Were Meant for Me; Good Morning; Would You?; Moses Supposes

featured song in this collection: Singin' in the Rain

Is there a better or more beloved movie musical than *Singin' in the Rain*? The title song, with Gene Kelly in a downpour dance, is possibly the most recognizable piece of film choreography. Producer Freed set out to build a story around old songs by Brown and himself, and with Comden & Green he wound up with one of the best scripts ever to bless a screen musical. Set in the late 1920s, as silent films were switching to sound, Kelly plays a movie star, Jean Hagen plays the silent star with a sqeaky voice, and Debbie Reynolds plays the singer/actress who dubs Hagen's songs and lines. In one of the great ironies in movie history, Reynolds' singing voice is also dubbed in a few spots in this movie. And if that isn't enough, in the plot when Reynolds is dubbing the speaking lines for Hagen, it's actually Hagen dubbing the lines for Reynolds dubbing the lines for Hagen, if you can figure that out. Reynolds' edgy twang wasn't right for the cultured dubbed voice needed, but Hagen, queen of squeak, could produce mellow tones much better than Debbie. That's Hollywood! The song "Singin' in the Rain" was introduced in the screen musical *Hollywood Revue of 1929*. Available on video.

THE SOUND OF MUSIC

1965, 20th Century-Fox

music by Richard Rodgers; lyrics by Oscar Hammerstein II; screenplay by Ernest Lehman; produced and directed by Robert Wise; choreography by Marc Breaux & DeeDee Wood; photography by Ted McCord

major cast members: Julie Andrews, Christopher Plummer, Eleanor Parker, Richard Haydn, Peggy Wood, Charmian Carr, Bil Baird Marionettes, Anna Lee, Portia Nelson, Marni Nixon, Daniel Truhitte, Norma Varden, Evadne Baker

songs: The Sound of Music; How Do You Solve a Problem Like Maria; I Have Confidence in Me (lyric: Richard Rodgers); Sixteen Going on Seventeen; My Favorite Things; Do Re Mi; Lonely Goatherd; Edelweiss; So Long, Farewell; How Can Love Survive?; Climb Ev'ry Mountain; Something good (lyric: Rodgers)

featured song in this collection: I Have Confidence in Me

The Sound of Music was the sixth and final Rodgers and Hammerstein stage musical to make it to the screen. Based on the true story of the Von Trapp family and their forced exile from their native Austria (thanks to Nazi tyranny), the film was the team's biggest money-maker and the only one of their screen treatments to win a best picture Academy Award (Robert Wise also won for his direction). Julie Andrews, fresh off her Oscar-winning performance the year before in **Mary Poppins**, was cast as Maria (Mary Martin played the role in the 1959 stage version), the governess who tames seven children and wins the heart of the autocratic father of the brood, Captain Georg Van Trapp (Christopher Plummer). Three of the original songs in the score were cut from the film, though two new ones with words and music by Rodgers were added, including "I Have Confidence in Me," sung by Andrews as she's about to begin her assignment as nanny to the Von Trapp children. Available on video.

SOUTH PACIFIC
1958, Magna

music by Richard Rodgers; lyrics by Oscar Hammerstein II; screenplay by Paul Osborn; produced by Buddy Adler; directed by Joshua Logan; choreography by LeRoy Prinz; photography by Leon Shamroy

major cast members: Rossano Brazzi, Mitzi Gaynor, John Kerr, Ray Walston, Juanita Hall, France Nuyen, Russ Brown, Ken Clark, Floyd Simmons, Candace Lee, Warren Hsieh, Archie Savage, Jack Mullaney, Beverly Aadland, Tom Laughlin

songs: Bloody Mary; There is Nothin' Like a Dame; Bali Ha'i; A Cock-Eyed Optimist; Twin Soliloquies; Some Enchanted Evening; Dites-moi (Tell Me Why); I'm Gonna Wash That Man Right Outa My Hair; A Wonderful Guy; Younger Than Springtime; Happy Talk; Honey Bun; My Girl Back Home; You've Got to Be Carefully Taught; This Nearly Was Mine

featured song in this collection: I'm Gonna Wash That Man Right Outa My Hair

South Pacific was another big budget, big screen treatment of a Rodgers and Hammerstein stage musical. Faithful to the 1949 stage production, the screen version retained the entire score, including "My Girl Back Home," which was cut prior to the Broadway opening. Based on two stories from James Michener's *Tales of the South Pacific*, two romantic tales are set against an exotic South Seas island during World War II. One involves the naive girl from Little Rock, Nellie Forbush (Mitzi Gaynor) and a widowed French planter Emile de Becque (Rossano Brazzi). The second romance is between young Lt. Joe Cable (John Kerr) and Liat (France Nuyen), the daughter of the Polynesian native Bloody Mary (Juanita Hall). The story throws in a strong message about racial intolerance. When Gaynor first discovers that Brazzi has two young Polynesian children, she abandons him and rationalizes her decision with the song "I'm Gonna Wash That Man Right Outa My Hair." The most peculiar part of the film is director Joshua Logan's mood altering use of colored filters during the outdoor musical numbers. Available on video.

STAR SPANGLED RHYTHM
1942, Paramount

music by Harold Arlen; lyrics by Johny Mercer; screenplay by Harry Tugend; produced by Joseph Sistrom; directed by George Marshall; choreography by Danny Dare, George Balanchine; photography by Leo Tover

major cast members: Bing Crosby, Bob Hope, Fred MacMurray, Franchot Tone, Ray Milland, Victor Moore, Dorothy Lamour, Paulette Goddard, Vera Zorina, Mary Martin, Dick Powell, Betty Hutton, Eddie Bracken, Veronica Lake, Alan Ladd, Eddie "Rochester" Anderson, William Bendix, Jerry Colonna, Macdonald Carey, Walter Abel, Susan Hayward, Marjorie Reynolds, Dona Drake, Lynne Overman, Johnnie Johnston, Gil Lamb, Cass Daley, Sterling Holloway, Ernest Truex, Katherine Dunham, Arthur Treacher, Walter Catlett, Golden Gate Quartet, Cecil B. DeMille, Preston Sturges

songs: Hit the Road to Dreamland; On the Swing Shift; I'm Doing it For Defense; A Sweater, a Sarong, and a Peek-a-boo Bang; That Old Black Magic; Old Glory

featured song in this collection: Hit the Road to Dreamland

World War II spawned a series of patriotic, flag-waving films. They went by such titles as *Stage Door Canteen, Thousands Cheer* and *Four Jills and Jeep.* To aid the war effort, all the major studios produced these high-budget extravaganzas. *Star Spangled Rhythm* was Paramount's tribute to the armed forces, featuring its own army of contract players. Like a giant vaudeville show, the film features various stars in a variety of comic sketches, blackouts and musical numbers. Victor Moore keeps the story moving with his portrayal of a studio guard who schemes with the switchboard operator (Betty Hutton) to secure the entire Paramount roster for a benefit show. Musically, *Star Spangled Rhythm* delivered with two Harold Arlen-Johnny Mercer hits, "That Old Black Magic" and "Hit the Road to Dreamland," introduced on a train by Mary Martin and Dick Powell.

STATE FAIR
1945, 20th Century-Fox

music by Richard Rodgers; lyrics by Oscar Hammerstein II; screenplay by Oscar Hammerstein II; produced by William Perlberg; directed by Walter Lang; photography by Leon Shamroy major cast members: Jeanne Crain, Dana Andrews, Dick Haymes, Vivian Blaine, Charles Winninger, Fay Bainter, Donald Meek, Frank McHugh, Percy Kilbride, Harry Morgan, William Marshall

songs: Our State Fair; It Might As Well Be Spring; It's a Grand Night for Singing; That's for Me; Isn't It Kinda Fun?; All I Owe Ioway

featured song in this collection: It Might As Well Be Spring

Rodgers and Hammerstein had pinned down a new musical/dramatic popular aesthetic in *Oklahoma!* of 1943, one utterly at odds with the New York, witty, casual, sophisticated tone set in the 1930s Broadway shows by the Gershwins, Cole Porter, and Lorenz Hart with Richard Rodgers himself, as well as the Astaire-Rogers film musicals. But a country at war didn't want wisecracking sophisticates on screen—it wanted simpler representations of pure Americana, morally righteous, and add quite a bit of sentiment, please. In *State Fair,* the only original movie musical by Rodgers and Hammerstein, the story keeps the rural musical plan, but updates it to present day Iowa. A farm family, with 2 young adult children, go to Des Moines to the big event of the year: camping out at the State Fair and showing their prize livestock, canned goods, and other homespun wares. The daughter and son both meet city slickin' love partners at the fair, and both get their hearts a little roughed up. There is a nightclub scene (at the Iowa State Fair!) with dancers and singers and people dressed up as if they were asked to be extras in a movie! No bermuda shorts and straw hats here! The lovely stand-out song, "It Might As Well Be Spring" is sung by Crain in her bedroom in the farmhouse before the trip to Des Moines. (Her singing was dubbed by Louanne Hogan). The musical was remade in 1962, this time changing the locale to the Texas State Fair, and starred Pat Boone and Ann-Margaret. Available on video.

● ● ● ● ● ● ● ● ● ● ● ● ● ●

STORMY WEATHER
1943, 20th Century-Fox

screenplay by Frederick Jackson & Ted Koehler; produced by William LeBaron; directed by Andrew Stone; choreography by Clarence Robinson, Nick Castle; photography by Leon Shamroy, Fred Sersen

major cast members: Bill Robinson, Lena Horne, Cab Calloway & Orch., Fats Waller, Katherin Dunham Dancers, Nicholas Brothers, Dooley Wilson, Flournoy Miller, Ada Brown, Zutty Singleton, Benny Carter, Babe Wallace

songs: There's No Two Ways About Love (J.P. Johnson-Ted Koehler); That Ain't Right (Nat King Cole-Irving Mills); Ain't Misbehavin' (Fats Waller, Harry Brooks-Andy Razaf); Diga Diga Doo (Jimmy McHugh-Dorothy Fields); Geechee Joe (Cab Calloway); Stormy Weather (Harold Arlen-Koehler); My My, Ain't That Somethin'? (Pinky Tomlin-Harry Tobias)

featured song in this collection: Stormy Weather

It was purported to be the story of legendary hoofer Bill "Bojangles" Robinson. But **Stormy Weather** was really a thinly-plotted backstager that gave the country's finest black entertainers an ample opportunity to showcase their specialities. The film features the dazzling dancing of the Nicholas Brothers, the keyboard versatility of Fats Waller and the exuberant singing of Cab Calloway. The story concerns Robinson (in his only starring role) and his pursuit of Lena Horne, from the end of World War I until the early '40s. The film was one of a handful (*Cabin in the Sky* and *Hallelujah* were two others) produced during this period by the major studios exclusively featuring black performers. *Stormy Weather* was also notable for its performance (by the sultry Horne) of the title song, written by Harold Arlen and Ted Koehler in 1933. Available on video.

● ● ● ● ● ● ● ● ● ● ● ● ● ●

SUMMER STOCK

1950, MGM

music by Harry Warren; lyrics by Mack Gordon; screenplay by George Wells, Sy Gomberg; produced by Joe Pasternak; directed by Charles Walters; choreography by Nick Castle (Gene Kelly, Charles Walters uncredited); photography by Robert Planck

major cast members: Judy Garland, Gene Kelly, Eddie Bracken, Gloria DeHaven, Marjorie Main, Phil Silvers, Ray Collins, Carleton Carpenter, Hans Conried, Carol Haney

songs: Happy Harvest; If You Feel Like Singing, Sing; You Wonderful You (lyric: Jack Brooks, Saul Chaplin); Friendly Star; Heavenly Music (Chaplin); Get Happy (Harold Arlen-Ted Koehler)

featured song in this collection: Get Happy

Let's put on a show in the barn! Sounds like an old Judy Garland-Mickey Rooney musical, doesn't it? Rooney's contract with MGM was terminated after **Words and Music** so the studio reteamed Garland with Gene Kelly for the third and final time. The backstage story was nothing new, but the magnetism between the two stars rises above the material. What the film does have is an above-average score by Harry Warren and Mack Gordon and some superb dance routines, particularly Kelly's imaginative "squeaky-board" number. Comic relief is provided by Kelly's **Cover Girl** sidekick Phil Silvers. Health problems caused Garland's weight to fluctuate wildly during filming. After initial photography for **Summer Stock** was completed, producer Joe Pasternak expressed concern that the film lacked a real show-stopper. Two months later and back from a stay in a sanitarium, Garland returned to shoot the classic Harold Arlen-Ted Koehler number "Get Happy." It was an ironic swan song for the now "fit" Garland. After 27 films MGM did not renew her contract. Available on video.

SWING TIME

1936, RKO Radio Pictures

music by Jerome Kern; lyrics by Dorothy Fields; screenplay by Howard Lindsay & Allan Scott; produced by Pandro S. Berman; directed by George Stevens; choreography by Hermes Pan (Fred Astaire uncredited); photography by David Abel

major cast members: Fred Astaire, Ginger Rogers, Victor Moore, Helen Broderick, Eric Blore, Betty Furness, George Metaxa, Landers Stevens, Frank Jenks, Ferdinand Munier, John Harrington, Pierre Watkin, Gerald Hamer, Edgar Dearing

songs: Pick Yourself Up; The Way You Look Tonight; Waltz in Swing Time (instrumental); A Fine Romance; Bojangles of Harlem; Never Gonna Dance

featured song in this collection: The Way You Look Tonight

For Depression-scarred movie audiences, the Fred Astaire-Ginger Rogers films were 100 minutes of pure escapism. Whether it was the opulent setting in **Top Hat** or the gritty life of the Navy in **Follow the Fleet**, moviegoers couldn't get enough of their favorite dance team. In their sixth teaming, **Swing Time**, Astaire plays a happy-go-lucky hoofer (and gambler nicknamed Lucky) who courts dance instructor Rogers. Comic relief is provided by Helen Broderick and Victor Moore. The score by Jerome Kern and Dorothy Fields produced a number of standards, including the Oscar-winning "The Way You Look Tonight." Astaire sings the song while playing the piano in Rogers' hotel room. The camera cuts to a close-up of Rogers in the bathroom, her hair lathered in shampoo. The film's masterpiece is Astaire's breathtaking tribute to dancer Bill Robinson, "Bojangles of Harlem," displaying the dancer at his creative zenith. Available on video.

THERE'S NO BUSINESS LIKE SHOW BUSINESS

1954, 20th Century-Fox

music & lyrics by Irving Berlin; screenplay by Henry & Phoebe Ephron; produced by Sol C. Siegel; directed by Walter Lang; choreography by Robert Alton, Jack Cole; photography by Leon Shamroy

major cast members: Ethel Merman, Donald O'Connor, Marilyn Monroe, Dan Dailey, Johnnie Ray, Mitzi Gaynor, Hugh O'Brian, Frank McHugh, Lee Patrick, Chick Chandler, Lyle Talbot

songs: When the Midnight Choo-Choo Leaves for Alabam'; Play a Simple Melody; After You Get What You Want You Don't Want It; A Man Chases a Girl (Until She Catches Him); You'd Be Surprised; Heat Wave; Alexander's Ragtime Band

featured song in this collection: Heat Wave

MGM was unequaled when it came to showcasing its stable of stars in thin-plotted musical revues that paid homage to popular American songwriters. Now, it was Fox's turn with **There's No Business Like Show Business**. After Ethel Merman's success in the screen version of **Call Me Madam**, studio chief Darryl Zanuck signed her to appear in another Irving Berlin musical. The title number was first introduced by Merman on Broadway in **Annie Get Your Gun**. The film follows the life of a show business family, headed by Merman and Dan Daily and their three talented offspring (Donald O'Connor, Mitzi Gaynor, and Johnnie Ray). The film consists of 12 Berlin standards and two new songs. Marilyn Monroe was cast as O'Connor's love interest and delivers a red hot rendition of "Heat Wave." Available on video.

● ● ● ● ● ● ● ● ● ● ● ● ● ● ● ● ● ●

TILL THE CLOUDS ROLL BY
1946, MGM

music by Jerome Kern, lyrics by Oscar Hammerstein II; screenplay by Myles Connolly & Jean Holloway; produced by Arthur Freed; directed by Richard Whorf, Vincente Minnelli (George Sidney uncredited); choreography by Robert Alton; photography by Harry Stradling, George Folsey

major cast members: June Allyson, Lucille Bremer, Judy Garland, Kathryn Grayson, Van Heflin, Lena Horne, Van Johnson, Tony Martin, Dinah Shore, Frank Sinatra, Robert Walker, Gower Champion, Cyd Charisse, Angela Lansbury, Ray McDonald, Virginia O'Brien, Dorothy Patrick, Caleb Peterson, Wilde Twins, Sally Forrest

songs: Make Believe; Can't Help Lovin' dat Man; Ol' Man River; How'd You Like to Spoon With Me? (lyric: Edward Laska); They Didn't Believe Me (lyric: M.E. Rourke); Till the Clouds Roll By (lyric: P.G. Wodehouse); Look for the Silver Lining (lyric: B.G. DeSylva); Who?; I Won't Dance (lyric: Dorothy Fields); Smoke Gets in Your Eyes (lyric: Otto Harbach); The Last Time I Saw Paris; Long Ago and Far Away (lyric: Ira Gershwin); All the Things You Are; Why Was I Born?

featured song in this collection: How'd You Like to Spoon With Me?

They were called musical biographies, films like **Rhapsody in Blue** (George Gershwin) and **Night and Day** (Cole Porter) set the stage for MGM's extravaganza, **Till The Clouds Roll By**.

This one paid homage to Jerome Kern. This very loosely based story on American popular songwriter Kern was really an excuse for MGM to roll out its roster of musical talent. The dialogue featuring Robert Walker as Kern was used as a bridge for the musical numbers. Kern's greatest stage triumph, **Show Boat** is given plenty of play with a 15-minute condensation, featuring Tony Martin, Kathryn Grayson (who would later star in the 1951 film version), Virginia O'Brien and Lena Horne. The film's oddity remains Frank Sinatra's interpretation of the classic, "Ol' Man River." Standing on a pedestal, bedecked in a white tuxedo and sporting a bouffant hairdo, it's a ludicrous finale. A young import from Britain, Angela Lansbury, is also featured, singing, "How'd You Like to Spoon With Me?" MGM gave similar screen treatments to Rodgers and Hart (**Words and Music**) and Sigmund Romberg (**Deep in My Heart**). None of the movies in this genre are exactly definitive biographies. Hollywood liberties abound. Available on video.

● ● ● ● ● ● ● ● ● ● ● ● ● ● ● ● ● ●

TOP HAT
1935, RKO Radio Pictures

music & lyrics by Irving Berlin; screenplay by Dwight Taylor & Allan Scott; produced by Pandro S. Berman; directed by Mark Sandrich; choreography by Hermes Pan (Fred Astaire uncredited); photography by David Abel

major cast members: Fred Astaire, Ginger Rogers, Edward Everett Horton, Helen Broderick, Erik Rhodes, Eric Blore, Lucille Ball, Leonard Mudie, Edgar Norton

songs: No Strings; Isn't This a Lovely Day?; Top Hat, White Tie and Tails; Cheek to Cheek; The Piccolino

featured song in this collection: Cheek to Cheek

The fourth Astaire-Rogers film, **Top Hat** bears a striking resemblance to their earlier success, **The Gay Divorcee** — affluent European locales, a mistaken identity, and a wacky supporting cast that formed the nucleus of an Astaire-Rogers stock company (Edward Everett Horton, Eric Blore, Erik Rhodes and Helen Broderick). Astaire plays an American dancer traveling abroad who falls in love with fellow American Rogers. Astaire woos her in a gazebo during a driving rain storm. Astaire sings, "Isn't This a Lovely Day?" and then slowly brings her into the dance routine. A few plot twists later, Astaire loses the girl before winning her back at the end. **Top Hat** is considered the quintessential Astaire-Rogers film, due in large part to Irving Berlin's melodious score, including the Astaire signature piece, "Top Hat, White Tie and Tails." The team's duet "Cheek to Cheek" remains an Astaire-Rogers classic, a number almost as famous for the behind-the-scenes problems caused by Rogers' feathered dress (which kept moulting during the filming) as the final results on the screen. Available on video.

WHITE CHRISTMAS

1954, Paramount

music & lyrics: Irving Berlin; screenplay by Norman Krasna, Norman Panama, Melvin Frank; produced by Robert Dolan; directed by Michael Curtiz; choreography by Robert Alton; photography by Loyal Griggs

major cast members: Bing Crosby, Danny Kaye, Rosemary Clooney, Vera-Ellen, Dean Jagger, Grady Sutton, Sig Rumann, Barrie Chase, George Chakiris

songs: White Christmas; The Old Man; Blue Skies; Sisters; The Best Things Happen While You're Dancing; Snow; Mandy; Count Your Blessings Instead of Sheep; Love, You Didn't Do Right by Me

featured song in this collection: Count Your Blessings Instead of Sheep

With a title like "White Christmas" how could it miss? The song had been a hit for 12 years when the movie came out, originally written for the 1942 musical *Holiday Inn*, starring Bing Crosby and Fred Astaire. The 1954 reunion of Berlin and Crosby was missing only one key ingredient — Astaire. Despite his absence (he took sick and was replaced by Danny Kaye), the film was a financial smash. The plot (vaguely reminiscent of *Holiday Inn*) tells the story of a successful song-and-dance team (Crosby and Kaye) who become romantically involved with two singing sisters (Rosemary Clooney and Vera-Ellen) and follow the girls to a resort in Vermont. While there, they discover that the inn is owned by their former commanding officer (Dean Jagger) who's in dire financial straits. Crosby and Kaye arrange to bring their whole Broadway revue to the resort in an effort to bail out the general. Crosby even makes an impassioned plea on a national television show to all their old army buddies to spend Christmas Eve at the inn. Sprinkled with a few Berlin standards such as the title tune and "Blue Skies," only one new song became popular, "Count Your Blessing Instead of Sheep," sung by Crosby. Available on video.

WHOOPEE!

1930, United Artists

music by Walter Donaldson; lyrics by Gus Kahn; screenplay by William Conselman; produced by Samuel Goldwyn, Florenz Ziegfeld; directed by Thornton Freeland; choreography by Busby Berkeley; photography by Lee Garmes, Ray Rennahan, Gregg Toland

major cast members: Eddie Cantor, Eleanor Hunt, Paul Gregory, Ethel Shutta, John Rutherford, Spencer Charters, Chief Caupolican, Albert Hackett, Marian Marsh, Betty Grable, Virginia Bruce, George Olsen Orch.

songs: I'll Still Belong to You (Nacio Herb Brown-Edward Eliscu); Makin' Whoopee; A Girl Friend of a Boy Friend of Mine; Stetson; My Baby Just Cares for Me; Song of the Setting Sun

featured song in this collection: Makin' Whoopee!

Long before Michelle Pfeiffer caused a sensation singing atop a piano in *The Fabulous Baker Boys*, bug-eyed comedian Eddie Cantor introduced the song "Makin' Whoopee" in the 1928 Broadway show, *Whoopee!* In need of cash, producer Florenz Ziegfeld sold the screen rights to Samuel Goldwyn, who promptly closed the show. Cantor began a six-film collaboration with Goldwyn and recreated the part of hypochondriac Henry Miller, who escapes to California for his health. Although only three of the original 13 songs were retained, this early sound film (shot in two-strip Technicolor) looks like a filmed stage play. *Whoopee!* gives Cantor plenty of room for his schtick, which he had honed during years on the vaudeville circuit. Song and production numbers emerge spontaneously, with little connection to the plot. Even the best known song, "Makin' Whoopee," is a film non sequitur, with Cantor singing, accompanied by a bevy of chorus girls. The film was also choreographer Busby Berkeley's first screen assignment. Available on video.

THE WIZARD OF OZ
1939, MGM

music by Harold Arlen; lyrics by E. Y. Harburg; secreenplay by Noel Langley, Florence Ryerson, Edgar Allan Woolf (John Lee Mahin, uncredited); produced by Mervyn LeRoy; directed by Victor Fleming (King Vidor, uncredited), choreography by Bobby Connolly; photography by Harold Rosson, Allen Darby

major cast members: Judy Garland, Frank Morgan, Ray Bolger, Bert Lahr, Jack Haley, Billie Burke, Margaret Hamilton, Charley Grapewin, Clara Blandick

songs: Over the Rainbow; Ding-Dong! The Witch Is Dead; Lullaby League and Lollypop Guild; Munchkinland; Optimistic Voices; We're Off to See the Wizard; Follow the Yellow Brick Road; If I Only Had a Brain; The Merry Old Land of Oz; If I Were King of the Forest

featured song in this collection: If I Only Had a Brain

Perhaps the most enduring and resonant original movie musical ever made. There are few pieces of popular art in the American culture that have risen to the level of icons, but *The Wizard of Oz* is certainly one. The movie is based on the book by Frank Baum, written in 1900. The story had been been musicalized on Broadway in 1903. How the movie came to be made is a tangled story of rights bought and sold, of 5 directors, a screenplay doctored up by many, and lots of other things tugging at the project's success. It is widely known that MGM desperately wanted Fox's Shirley Temple to play the role of Dorothy (one doesn't like to ponder too long what that would have been like), and only settled for Garland from their own lot when the negotiations with Fox reached an impass. The finished film is so seamless that it shows absolutely none of the turbulance of the project's development. The movie made Garland an unqualified star, and her singing of "Over the Rainbow" (almost cut from the movie 3 different times) is one of the high points of her long screen career. The Scarecrow's snappy lament, "If I Only Had a Brain," is later taken up by his colleagues, the Tin Woodman and the Cowardly Lion. Available on video.

WORDS AND MUSIC
1948, MGM

music by Richard Rodgers; lyrics by Lorenz Hart; screenplay by Fred Finklehoffe; produced by Arthur Freed; directed by Norman Taurog; choreography by Robert Alton, Gene Kelly; photography by Charles Rosher, Harry Stradling

major cast members: June Allyson, Perry Como, Judy Garland, Lena Horne, Gene Kelly, Mickey Rooney, Ann Sothern, Tom Drake, Cyd Charisse, Betty Garrett, Janet Leigh, Marshall Thompson, Mel Tormé, Vera-Ellen, Richard Quine, Dee Turnell; Allyn Ann McLerie, Blackburn Twins, Clinton Sundberg

songs: Manhattan; There's a Small Hotel; Mountain Greenery; Where's That Rainbow?; On Your Toes; Thou Swell; Where or When; The Lady Is a Tramp; I Wish I Were in Love Again; Johnny One Note; Blue Moon; Spring is Here; Slaughter on Tenth Avenue (instrumental); With a Song in My Heart

featured song in this collection: Thou Swell

Accuracy was not of primary concern when MGM filmed the life stories of composers Jerome Kern (*Till the Clouds Roll By*) and Sigmund Romberg (*Deep in My Heart*). The songwriting team of Richard Rodgers and Lorenz Hart received the biographical musical treatment in *Words and Music*. These films were more an excuse to showcase the studio's stars. *Words and Music* traces the team's career with Rodgers (Tom Drake) providing the sturdy balance to the bombastic Hart (Mickey Rooney). The film uses 17 Rodgers & Hart songs. Highlights include two numbers by Judy Garland, "I Wish I Were in Love Again" (her last on-screen duet with Rooney) and "Johnny One Note," two solos by Lena Horne, and June Allyson cavorting with the Blackburn Twins in "Thou Swell." Nothing beats the intensity of "The Slaughter on Tenth Avenue" ballet, featuring Gene Kelly and Vera-Ellen. The film ends with Rooney's zombie-like death march down a Broadway alley during a pouring rain. The cause of Hart's tragic death at age 48? According to the film, it was his unrequited love for a nightclub singer, played by Betty Garrett. It was actually brought on by decades of drinking. Available on video.

● ●

YANKEE DOODLE DANDY

1942, Warner Brothers

music & lyrics by George M. Cohan; screenplay by Robert Bruckner & Edmund Joseph (Julius & Philip Epstein uncredited); produced by Hal B. Wallis; directed by Michael Curtiz; choreography by LeRoy Prinz, Seymour Felix, John Boyle; photography by James Wong Howe

major cast members: James Cagney, Joan Leslie, Walter Huston, Richard Whorf, Irene Manning, George Tobias, Rosemary DeCamp, Jeanne Cagney, Frances Langford, George Barbier, S.Z. Sakall, Walter Catlett, Eddie Foy Jr., Odette Myrtil, Charles Smith, Georgia Carroll, Leslie Brooks, Spencer Charters

songs: I Was Born in Virginia; Harrigan; The Yankee Doodle Boy; Give My Regards to Broadway; Oh, You Wonderful Girl; I'll Be True to You; Belle of the Barbers' Ball; Mary's a Grand Old Name; Forty-Five Minutes from Broadway; So Long, Mary; You're a Grand Old Flag; Over There

featured song in this collection: Give My Regards to Broadway

Warner Brothers, sensing the patriotic fervor sweeping the nation just prior to World War II, spared no expense in bringing the life story of George M. Cohan to the screen. *Yankee Doodle Dandy* is the sentimental, flag-waving story of one of Broadway's most colorful characters. From vaudeville hoofer, dramatist, actor, producer, songwriter and unabashed patriot, Cohan was perfectly portrayed by James Cagney (Cohan's personal choice for the role) in an Academy Award winning performance. Cagney brought his own nuances to the part, while capturing the brash, sentimental and serious side of Cohan. It's an electrifying performance — and the only one Cagney would later take pride in. The film traces Cohan from struggling hoofer with his family's vaudeville act to the recipient of the Congressional Medal of Honor. Known more for his gangster roles, Cagney (who began his career as a hoofer) perfectly captured Cohan's stiff-legged tap dance style. Although no real competition for Astaire and Kelly, the energetic Cagney struts his stuff during an 11-minute version of Cohan's *Little Johnny Jones*, featuring "The Yankee Doodle Boy" and "Give My Regards to Broadway." Available on video.

● ●

YOUNG AT HEART

1955, Warner Brothers

screenplay adaptation by Liam O'Brien (from screenplay "Four Daughters" by Julius Epstein & Lenore Coffee); produced by Henry Blanke, directed by Gordon Douglas; photography by Ted McCord

major cast members: Frank Sinatra, Doris Day, Gig Young, Ethel Barrymore, Dorothy Malone, Robert Keith, Elisabeth Fraser, Alan Hale Jr., Lonny Chapman, Frank Ferguson, Majorie Bennet, John Maxwell, William McLean, Barbara Pepper, Robin Raymond

songs: Young at Heart (Johnny Richards-Carolyn Leigh); Someone to Watch Over me (George & Ira Gershwin); Just One of Those Things (Cole Porter); One for My Baby (Harold Arlen-Johnny Mercer); You, My Love (Mack Gordon-James Van Heusen)

featured song in this collection: Young at Heart

Considered more a musical-drama than musical-comedy, *Young at Heart* stars Frank Sinatra as Barney Sloan, a cynical arranger hired by a composer (Gig Young) to assist him in writing a Broadway musical. He soon falls in love with one of the daughters in the household (Doris Day), although she is already engaged to someone else. Forlorn, Sinatra attempts to kill himself by driving his car off the road. (The role was probably not a real stretch for Sinatra, who at the time was distraught over his separation from wife Ava Gardner.) The overly romantic story, common to movies of the 1950's, is put into a slick package and made enjoyable by the singing of Sinatra and Day. The film is the musical adaptation of *Four Daughters*, a 1938 film directed by Michael Curtiz and starring John Garfield in his feature film debut. Available on video.

● ●

LOVE IS HERE TO STAY

from AN AMERICAN IN PARIS

Music and Lyrics by
GEORGE and IRA GERSHWIN

Lively

The more I read the pa-pers The less I com-pre-hend The

world and all its ca-pers And how it all will end.

Noth-ing seems to be last-ing, But that is-n't our af-fair;

ANYTHING YOU CAN DO

from ANNIE GET YOUR GUN

Words and Music by
IRVING BERLIN

THAT'S ENTERTAINMENT
from THE BAND WAGON

Words by HOWARD DIETZ
Music by ARTHUR SCHWARTZ

JUST IN TIME

from BELLS ARE RINGING

Words by BETTY COMDEN and ADOLPH GREEN
Music by JULE STYNE

THANKS FOR THE MEMORY

from the Paramount Picture THE BIG BROADCAST OF 1938

Words and Music by LEO ROBIN
and RALPH RAINGER

MONEY, MONEY
from CABARET

Lyric by FRED EBB
Music by JOHN KANDER

(I WONDER WHY?)
YOU'RE JUST IN LOVE

from CALL ME MADAM

Words and Music by
IRVING BERLIN

Your heart goes pit - ter pat - ter. I know just

what's the mat - ter, be - cause I've been there once _ or twice. _

F Gm7 G♭7♭5 F

Put your head

on my shoul - der. You need some - one who's old - er.

YOU DO SOMETHING TO ME

from CAN-CAN

Words and Music by
COLE PORTER

CHANGE PARTNERS

from the RKO Radio Motion Picture CAREFREE

Words and Music by
IRVING BERLIN

SOMETHING'S GOTTA GIVE

from DADDY LONG LEGS

Words and Music by
JOHNNY MERCER

A FOGGY DAY

from A DAMSEL IN DISTRESS

Words by IRA GERSHWIN
Music by GEORGE GERSHWIN

STEPPIN' OUT WITH MY BABY

from the Motion Picture Irving Berlin's EASTER PARADE

Words and Music by
IRVING BERLIN

CARIOCA
from FLYING DOWN TO RIO

Words by GUS KAHN and EDWARD ELISCU
Music by VINCENT YOUMANS

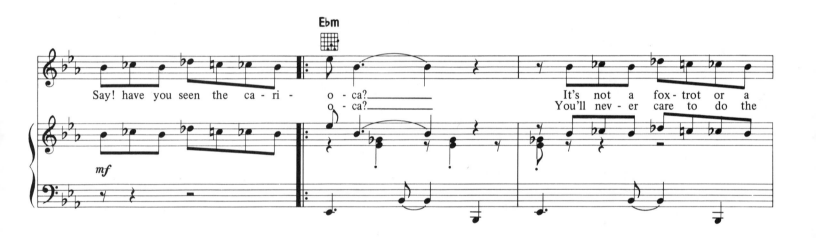

Say! have you seen the ca-ri - o - ca?_____
o - ca?_____

It's not a fox-trot or a
You'll nev - er care to do the

pol - ka,_____
pol - ka,_____

It has a lit - tle bit of new rhy-thm, a
And then you re - al-ize the blue hu - la and

FOR ME AND MY GAL

from FOR ME AND MY GAL

Words by EDGAR LESLIE and E. RAY GOETZ
Music by GEORGE W. MEYER

In his wed-ding ar - ray_____ Hear him smil-ing - ly say:_____
Gee! it makes the boy proud_____ As he says to the crowd:_____

Chorus:

"The bells are ring - ing_____ For Me And My Gal,_____

The birds are sing - ing_____ For Me And My Gal._____

___ Ev - 'ry - bod - y's been know - ing_____ To a wed-ding they're go - ing_____

And for weeks they've been sew - ing,_____ Ev - 'ry Su - sie and Sal._____

FUNNY GIRL

from FUNNY GIRL

Words by BOB MERRILL
Music by JULE STYNE

THE CONTINENTAL

from THE GAY DIVORCEE

Words by CON CONRAD
Music by HERBERT MAGIDSON

FORTY-SECOND STREET

from 42ND STREET

Words by AL DUBIN
Music by HARRY WARREN

TOO-RA-LOO-RA-LOO-RAL
(THAT'S AN IRISH LULLABY)

from GOING MY WAY

Words and Music by
J.R. SHANNON

I REMEMBER IT WELL

from GIGI

Words by ALAN JAY LERNER
Music by FREDERICK LOEWE

too?_____ That car-riage ride. *She:* You walked me home. *He:* You lost a

glove. *She:* I lost a comb. *He:* Ah yes! I re-mem-ber it well.

That bril-liant sky. *She:* We had some rain. *He:* Those Rus-sian songs. *She:* From sun-ny

Spain. *He:* Ah yes! I re-mem-ber it well. You

THE FOLKS WHO LIVE ON THE HILL

from HIGH, WIDE AND HANDSOME

Lyrics by OSCAR HAMMERSTEIN II
Music by JEROME KERN

ON THE ATCHISON, TOPEKA AND THE SANTA FE

from THE HARVEY GIRLS

Words by JOHNNY MERCER
Music by HARRY WARREN

TRUE LOVE

from HIGH SOCIETY

Words and Music by
COLE PORTER

Moderately Slow

I'LL CAPTURE YOUR HEART SINGING

from the Motion Picture Irving Berlin's HOLIDAY INN

Words and Music by
IRVING BERLIN

Cros - by sings __ pret - ty swell __ Fred A - staire __ dan - ces well __

I'm that com - bin - a - tion __ That's my re - pu - ta - tion. __

+) Symbols for Guitar, Chords for Ukulele and Banjo

YOU'RE JUST TOO TOO

from LES GIRLS

Words and Music by
COLE PORTER

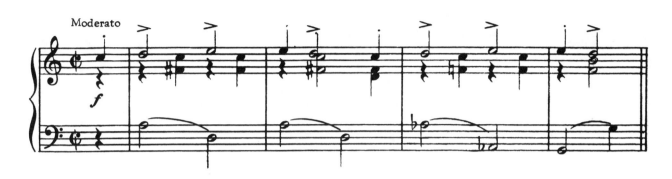

MY MAMMY

from THE JAZZ SINGER

Words by SAM M. LEWIS and JOE YOUNG
Music by WALTER DONALDSON

Moderately (with a light beat)

TOO DARN HOT

from KISS ME KATE

Words and Music by
COLE PORTER

Easy Fox-trot tempo

It's too darn hot. It's too darn hot. I'd like to sup ____ with my ba-by, to-night, ____ Re-fill the cup ____ with my ba-by to-night,

LOVE ME OR LEAVE ME

from LOVE ME OR LEAVE ME

Lyrics by GUS KAHN
Music by WALTER DONALDSON

less that some-one is you_____ I in-tend to be in-de-pend-ent-ly

blue._____ I want your love but I don't want to borrow to

have it to-day and to give back to-mor-row, For my love is your love, There's

no love for no-bod-y-else!_

ISN'T IT ROMANTIC?

from the Paramount Picture LOVE ME TONIGHT

Words by LORENZ HART
Music by RICHARD RODGERS

FEED THE BIRDS

from Walt Disney's MARY POPPINS

Words and Music by RICHARD M. SHERMAN
and ROBERT B. SHERMAN

Come feed the lit-tle birds, show them you care And you'll be glad if you do;_____ Their young ones are hun-gry, their nests are so bare; All it takes is tup-pence from you._____

CHORUS

Feed _____ the birds, tup-pence _____ a bag, Tup-pence, _____

UNDER THE BAMBOO TREE

from MEET ME IN ST. LOUIS

Words and Music by ROBERT COLE
and J. ROSAMOND JOHNSON

IT'S EASY TO REMEMBER

from the Paramount Picture MISSISSIPPI

Words by LORENZ HART
Music by RICHARD RODGERS

I'VE GROWN ACCUSTOMED TO HER FACE

from MY FAIR LADY

Words by ALAN JAY LERNER
Music by FREDERICK LOEWE

AH! SWEET MYSTERY OF LIFE
from NAUGHTY MARIETTA

Music by VICTOR HERBERT
Lyrics by RIDA JOHNSON YOUNG

PEOPLE WILL SAY WE'RE IN LOVE
from OKLAHOMA!

Lyrics by OSCAR HAMMERSTEIN II
Music by RICHARD RODGERS

NEW YORK, NEW YORK

from ON THE TOWN

Words by BETTY COMDEN and ADOLPH GREEN
Music by LEONARD BERNSTEIN

We've got___ one day___ here, and not an-oth-er
The fam-ous plac - es to vis-it are so
Man-hat-tan wom - en are dressed in silk and

min-ute to see the fa-mous sights;___
man - y, or so the guide-books say;___
sat - in, or so the fel-lows say;___

I COULD WRITE A BOOK

from PAL JOEY

Words by LORENZ HART
Music by RICHARD RODGERS

BE A CLOWN

from THE PIRATE

Words and Music by
COLE PORTER

SMOKE GETS IN YOUR EYES

from ROBERTA

Words by OTTO HARBACH
Music by JEROME KERN

ROSALIE
from ROSALIE

Words and Music by
COLE PORTER

175

SAN FRANCISCO

from SAN FRANCISCO

Words by GUS KAHN
Music by BRONISLAU KAPER and WALTER JURMANN

179

LET'S CALL THE WHOLE THING OFF

from SHALL WE DANCE

Music and Lyrics by
GEORGE and IRA GERSHWIN

Things have come to a pret-ty pass Our ro-mance is grow-ing flat, For

you like this and the oth-er__ While I go for this and that.

MAKE BELIEVE
from SHOW BOAT

Words by OSCAR HAMMERSTEIN II
Music by JEROME KERN

I'M GONNA WASH THAT MAN RIGHT OUTA MY HAIR

from SOUTH PACIFIC

Lyrics by OSCAR HAMMERSTEIN II
Music by RICHARD RODGERS

ALL OF YOU

from SILK STOCKINGS

Words and Music by
COLE PORTER

Fox Trot Tempo

With bounce, not too fast

Af - ter watch - ing her ap - peal from ev - 'ry an - gle, ____ ____ There's a big ro - man - tic deal I've got to wan - gle. ____ For I've fall - en for a

SINGIN' IN THE RAIN

from SINGIN' IN THE RAIN

Words by ARTHUR FREED
Music by NACIO HERB BROWN

Sing - in' In The Rain, Just Sing - in' In The Rain. What a glo - ri - ous feel - ing I'm hap - py a - gain, I'm

Why do I get up each morn-ing to start ____

Hap - py and het up with joy in my heart? ____

Why is each new task a tri - fle to do? ____ Be -

D. S. al Fine

cause I am liv - ing a life full of you. ____ I'm

I HAVE CONFIDENCE

from THE SOUND OF MUSIC

Lyrics and Music by
RICHARD RODGERS

HIT THE ROAD TO DREAMLAND

from the Paramount Picture STAR SPANGLED RHYTHM

Words by JOHNNY MERCER
Music by HAROLD ARLEN

★Chord Names For Guitar

STORMY WEATHER
(KEEPS RAININ' ALL THE TIME)
from STORMY WEATHER

Lyric by TED KOEHLER
Music by HAROLD ARLEN

IT MIGHT AS WELL BE SPRING

from STATE FAIR

Lyrics by OSCAR HAMMERSTEIN II
Music by RICHARD RODGERS

THE WAY YOU LOOK TONIGHT
from SWING TIME

Words by DOROTHY FIELDS
Music by JEROME KERN

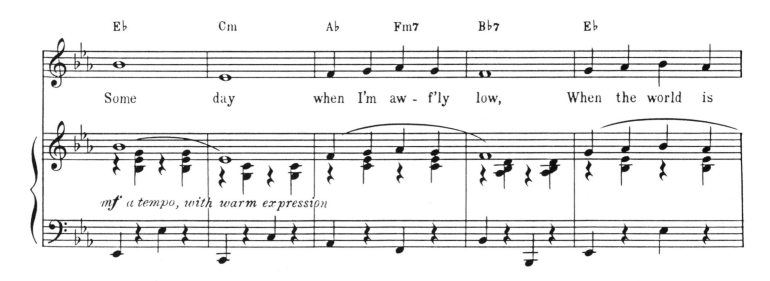

GET HAPPY

from SUMMER STOCK

Lyrics by TED KOEHLER
Music by HAROLD ARLEN

COUNT YOUR BLESSINGS INSTEAD OF SHEEP

from the Motion Picture Irving Berlin's WHITE CHRISTMAS

Words and Music by
IRVING BERLIN

HEAT WAVE

from THERE'S NO BUSINESS LIKE SHOW BUSINESS

Words and Music by
IRVING BERLIN

A heat wave blew right in - to town __ last week. __

She came from the

Is - land of Mar - tin - ique. __

Lyrics:

way that she moves ___ that ther-mo-me-ter proves ___ that she

cer-tain-ly can ___ can - can. We're can - can.

can - can. It's so hot the weath-er man will tell you

a re - cord's been made. ___

HOW'D YOU LIKE TO SPOON WITH ME

from TILL THE CLOUDS ROLL BY

Words by EDWARD LASKA
Music by JEROME KERN

CHEEK TO CHEEK
from the RKO Radio Motion Picture TOP HAT

Words and Music by
IRVING BERLIN

235

MAKIN' WHOOPEE!

from WHOOPEE!

Words by GUS KAHN
Music by WALTER DONALDSON

IF I ONLY HAD A BRAIN

from THE WIZARD OF OZ

Lyrics by E.Y. HARBURG
Music by HAROLD ARLEN

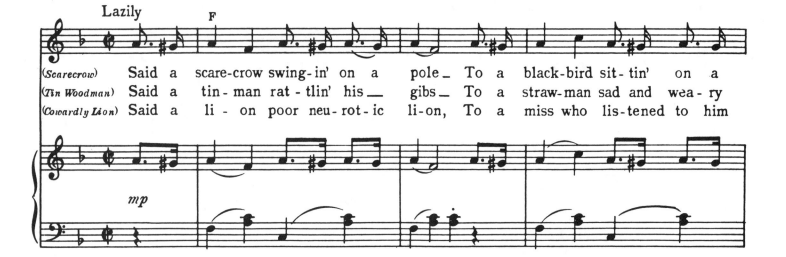

(Scarecrow) Said a scare-crow swing-in' on a pole To a black-bird sit-tin' on a
(Tin Woodman) Said a tin-man rat-tlin' his gibs To a straw-man sad and wea-ry
(Cowardly Lion) Said a li-on poor neu-rot-ic li-on, To a miss who lis-tened to him

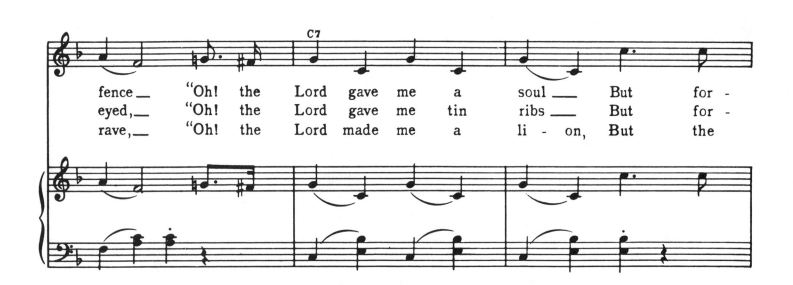

fence "Oh! the Lord gave me a soul But for-
eyed, "Oh! the Lord gave me tin ribs But for-
rave, "Oh! the Lord made me a li-on, But the

243

245

THOU SWELL
from WORDS AND MUSIC

Words by LORENZ HART
Music by RICHARD RODGERS

GIVE MY REGARDS TO BROADWAY

from YANKEE DOODLE DANDY

Words and Music by
GEORGE M. COHAN

YOUNG AT HEART

from YOUNG AT HEART

Words by CAROLYN LEIGH
Music by JOHNNY RICHARDS